THE NATURE OF KNOYLE

Detail of the Village Hall mural by Ronald Homes, depicting Sir Christopher Wren, Clouds House, the Windmill and the Wyndham daughters

The Nature of Knoyle

East Knoyle, the people and the place

ANTHONY CLAYDON

Linda and Neville.

Best Wishes.

Tony

1 November 2002

First published in the United Kingdom in 2002 by
The Hobnob Press, PO Box 1838, East Knoyle, Salisbury SP3 6FA

British Library Cataloguing in Publication Data
A catalogue record for this book is available from the British Library.

ISBN 0-946418-13-6

Typeset in 11/13.5 pt Souvenir Light
Typesetting and origination by John Chandler
Printed in Great Britain by Salisbury Printing Company Ltd, Salisbury

About the Author

ANTHONY CLAYDON was born in 1931 in the North West Frontier Province of what is now Pakistan. After leaving Tonbridge School, he was called up for National Service with the Royal Artillery. This led to a full thirty-year army career; during which he gained a Master of Letters degree from Lancaster University. He had a second career in the Civil Service until retiring in 1991.

Since coming to live in East Knoyle in 1978, he has developed a strong interest in the history and environment of the people of south-west Wiltshire. Married to Joan, with two grown-up children, his other interests include: fellwalking, rugby football, bellringing and yoga.

Contents

To Warminster

Pertwood

Upper Pertwood
Bushes

Bockerly
Hill

Knoyle Down

Tumuli

Long Barrow

Tumulus

Two Mile Down

To Mere

Celtic Fields

B.3089

Chapel Field
Barn

Tumulus

A.350

Chapel Fm.

Raked Field
Coppice

Clouds Hill
Close
Coppice

Upton

Haddon Hill

Sheephouse
Fm.

Moat
Shadmarsh House

The Green

Milton

Great Hall
Croft

Warminster

Mansltion

Windmill Hill

Clouds House

Knoyle Ridge

Combe Bottom

Vernhill
Fm.

Lugmarsh
Fm.

Holloway

Sandpit
Coppice

East Knoyle

el Moor's Fm.

Church
Leigh

Park
Coppice

King's Bushes

Great
Ground
Coppice

Alder
Common

Upper Leigh

Summerleaze
Fm.

Snaggs Fm.

Priors Hayes
Fm.

New Heaze
Fm.

Blackhouse
Fm.

Lower Leigh
Fm.

Redhouse
Fm.

River Sem

Wood

Parish Boundary

Footpaths & Bridle paths ------

Post Office   P

Trigonometrical Point.   △

Church with Tower

Windmill

Windpump

Ministry of Transport, Class 1

2

Introduction and Acknowledgements

This book is a story about East Knoyle and its people; ancient and modern. Except when there is a need to be specific in the text, it is generally described as 'Knoyle' for convenience. This is in the same way as the Seymour family called their mansion 'Knoyle House' and the Rectory became 'Knoyle Place' when it was sold by the Church to the Fison family in the 1930s.

No disrespect whatever is intended towards the equally ancient twin village of West Knoyle; whose boundaries were certified by royal charter in AD 948.

Where possible, attributions have been given in the notes to each chapter. The idea of writing this account was born when Mrs Janet Wharton and I set up the village photo and document archive nine years ago. It has only become a reality through the help, encouragement, documents, photographs and recollections of very many people both in the village and outside. To all of them I am enormously grateful.

It is only possible to list just a few of them here:

The late Mrs Alice Beard.
Mr Tom Biss
The late Alison Borthwick
Mrs Heather Bull
Mrs Clifford Burton
Mr Peter Chandler
Mr Michael Hull
Mr Richard Hyde
Mrs Winifred Hyde
Mrs Joan Jesse and her late husband John
Miss Marion Littlecott
Dr David Longbourne
Mr Peter Lucas

Mr John Maine RA
The Hon. Diana Makgill
Mr and Mrs 'Mick' Mickleburgh
Colonel Douglas Morris
The late Miss Rosemary Olivier
The Bishop of Ramsbury
Mr John Reading
The late Mrs Anne Ridler OBE
Mrs E.M. Roberts
The late Colonel Stephen Scammell
The late Mrs Jack Steedman
Mr and Mrs Clifford Sully
The late Mr Alfred Tanswell.
Mr Harry Wharton

I am very grateful to the donor, Miss Elizabeth Glen-Coats, the artist Mr Ron Homes and the East Knoyle Village Hall Management Committee for

Opposite page: Map of the parish of East Knoyle, circa 1955, drawn for the Women's Institute scrapbook (scale: 1.4 inches = 1 mile)

permission to photograph the village hall mural for the cover of this book..
Special thanks are due to Dr John Chandler for his practical help and
collaboration on local historical matters over the years – and in bringing this
work to fruition through the Hobnob Press. Finally, another special 'Thank
You' – to my wife. Without Joan's skilled help and constant encouragement
the book would never have seen the light of day.

Many sources have been consulted in researching this account. Some
of them conflict. In selecting the line to follow, there must be some risk that
errors of fact or of interpretation will creep in. If any have done so, I hope that
this will not spoil the reader's enjoyment.

Anthony Claydon
East Knoyle, 2002.

Beginnings

The Stone Age

The oldest object in our village is the sarsen stone just west of the upper part of the bypass. Scientists state that it is of glacial origin; but as folklore has it: 'They do say as Old Nick dropped it there, when he was carrying it to build Stonehenge'.[1] It has survived the efforts of horses and ropes to move it, and possibly stronger methods too. The new bypass left it unscathed, so we still have our reminder of the most distant past.

This picture of the Sarsen stone was taken before the coming of the bypass, which runs through the wood on the right

Dinosaur remains have been found just over the nearby county boundary with Dorset at Gillingham; so perhaps they may have roamed in our southern clays 100 million or so years ago.

The finding of 'paddle' bones suggests Plesiosaurus: about 15 feet long with a broad, flat body and short tail. Equipped with long, sharp teeth, it probably fed by swinging its head from side to side through a school of fish. It could use its paddle-like limbs to swim backwards or forwards or even to rotate itself around its body axis.

The first datable appearance of modern man here is in the New Stone Age (4500-2500 BC). There is a long barrow just north of the A303[2] and an axe head was found a bit further south.

The best evidence, however, came from the bottom of Windmill Hill. As reported in the *Wiltshire Archaeological & Natural History Magazine*:[3] In 1931 Mr Sales of Reading noticed a group of flint implements on the window sill of a house in East Knoyle. The finder, Mr Garrett,[4] gave them to Mr Sales, whose widow gave them to Reading Museum.

Whilst cutting bracken on the hillside of a small chalk and flint quarry, Mr Garrett noticed a patch of dark soil and dug into it. At a depth of three feet he found a pot about one foot in diameter and 15 inches high. The pottery was plain without any decoration. It crumbled to pieces and nothing of it remains. Close by was found a block of chert (flintlike quartz) and three implements. These were: a chipped and partly polished flint celt (a prehistoric cutting tool) of pointed oval section, probably used as an adze; a polished flint celt of oval section with slightly flattened sides; and lastly a sickle of bluish grey flint. This last is carefully flaked over the convex face, but the major part of the primary flake scar is untouched. The concave edge is sharp and has 1½ inches from the tip a large area of diffused gloss. In shape the sickle forms a fairly symmetrical curve and is the most westerly example of its kind found in England.

The three pieces now form part of a neolithic display in the Salisbury and South Wiltshire Museum. Though the available technology was quite

limited, the creation of stone artifacts, large and small, was often of high quality workmanship; while internal trading routes were evidently well established by this period. Excavations at Robin Hood's Ball, on the edge of the Larkhill Artillery Range, unearthed polished axes from the Langdale area of the Lake District and other artifacts from Cornwall.[5]

These carefully knapped Stone Age tools were found below the windmill, a few hundred metres from where Mr Garrett made his discovery.

A fine set of three neolithic tools and two associated offcuts was found recently on the surface to the Northwest of the windmill, just a few hundred yards from Mr Garrett's find. The artifacts have been authenticated, and kindly presented by the finder to the Village Archive.

The Bronze Age

A round 2500 BC long barrows went out of fashion as a new race of settlers began to arrive from the middle Rhine valley and the Low Countries. This race is known as the Beaker people from the distinctive pottery drinking vessels which they produced.

At first, they used flint implements like their predecessors. Later, however, they introduced skilled metalworking techniques whereby copper smelted with 12-15% tin produced bronze with a much harder edge. The higher figure gave a sharper blade, but was more brittle.

This Bronze Age axe head was broken in antiquity. It was found close to the A303 where there is a barrow grave.

Just north of the A303 a bronze axe head was found, which had been broken in antiquity. Near Upton a superbly worked arrow or small spear head 6cms long came to light. Its blades were still sharp and it had a barb on the tang . This is one of a type only rarely found in Britain and may have been imported. The British Museum has dated it to the later Bronze Age 1300-600 BC.

There was also a bronze palstave (the archaeologists' name given to a chisel edged instrument shaped to fit into a split handle) 17 cms long and finely

This superb arrow or small spear head came from the North of the parish. It is unusual in having a barb on the 'tang' or shaft, and is one of two so far found in Britain. It may have been imported across the English Channel. The British Museum has dated it to between BC 1300 and the end of the Bronze Age in about BC 600.

hammered. This was bought in London in about 1966 and was said to have come from East Knoyle.

Most significantly, work carried out by AC *archaeology* under Peter Cox discovered a ploughed-out burial mound c1500 BC just below the brow of the hill at the north end of the bypass. The siting would have been quite deliberate: so that the tomb of the obviously important person would have been at its most impressive to someone looking upwards from below – particularly in the early days when the chalk earthworks would have stood out from the surrounding turf. There may have been an outer ring bank; and if so, this would have been of the early Bronze Age. Unfortunately no primary (i.e. original) burial was found, so the tomb was probably robbed in ancient times.

It seems logical that this mound would have been near the centre of the farming community responsible for the Bronze Age cultivation system on either side of White's Lane, which runs from Park Farm to Milton. This was later used by the Celts and is still visible today.

The Iron Age

A round 600 BC the climate became wetter and colder. This caused some land to be taken out of cultivation; with consequent strong competition for the more fertile, usable soils.

Throughout central southern Britain hillforts were built to protect the people and their assets. These varied from large, complex and skilfully designed defensive sites like Maiden Castle and Hod Hill, both in modern Dorset, to simple constructions. There is thought to have been a hill fort on Two Mile Down.[6] If so it would have been one of the latter.

Some of the forts were not occupied for very long. In the earlier part of the period, vertical wooden defensive walls were built against the banks which were effective against an attacker but costly in men, materials and time to maintain. Later, it became more usual to rely on the steep earth banks without revetment. By about 100BC many forts were simply abandoned.

AC *archaeology's* survey for the Knoyle bypass discovered an Iron Age enclosure just below the Bronze Age burial mound, which must have been respected. There was a line of post holes at the northern end. After a bout of rain, a round hut was discovered, with its entrance towards the Southeast, to catch the best of the sun. Because the road scrape for the bypass only exposed a 'slice' through the settlement, its full extent is not known, but it lay within a ditched enclosure. As well as traces of other round huts, there were also cobbled working areas. There were a number of round holes which may have served as latrines, as well as storage pits – described in more detail below.

These reconstructed Iron Age round houses come from Henllys in Wales. The Knoyle hut was probably of similar construction, with its door facing south-east to catch the early morning sunlight.

Other finds included: A rotary quern for grinding corn, with both its top and bottom stones; Flat quern stones for the same purpose; Worked flint and stone weights for a loom or to hold down a thatched roof; Pottery; Iron and bronze metal-working slag, being a byproduct of smithing activity; Charred cereal grain.[7, 8] Taken as a whole, together with the field system originating in the Bronze age, these finds point to a largely self-sufficient farming community with a well established annual routine.

The community would not have been isolated from mainstream Celtic activity. There was a major trading route stretching from Devon to East Anglia. This made use of the high ground on hill features and has become known as the Great Ridgeway.

Although it is difficult to be certain of the exact alignment, Battlesbury Iron Age fort above Warminster lay alongside it, from where it led South through Sutton Veny. From there it went to Pertwood and along the line later chosen by the 18th-century builders of the East Knoyle to Warminster turnpike, now the A350. From Knoyle it was on to Ivy Cross, Shaftesbury. There was also possibly a loop from Pertwood by Chapel Field Barn and Chapel Farm, Windmill Hill and Holloway, before rejoining the main route.[9]

By the latter part of the first millennium BC, the inhabitants would have been Celts; though their Beaker people predecessors may not have entirely disappeared but have been absorbed into the newer culture.

The Celts were members of an Indo-European people first known in Europe about 1200 BC: in the basin of the upper Danube, the Alps, and parts of France and South Germany. Belgic tribes, of mixed Germanic and Celtic stock, came to inhabit northern Gaul and spread into southern Britain. Dorset became the territory of the Durotriges, with a main tribal centre at Maiden Castle near Dorchester but extending into South Wiltshire.

Because the British Celts had no written language of their own, until very recently people have relied on contemporary Roman authors such as Julius Caesar. They were writing with at least one eye on domestic political considerations. Their portrayals produced a stereotype of a ferocious 'battle-mad' race of barbarians, who dyed themselves bright blue before combat; using *Isatis tinctoria*, the Woad plant.

Their bravery was acknowledged, as well as their skill in guerrilla type warfare and chariot tactics (though the famous swords on the chariot wheels do not seem to have much foundation in fact). After battle, they were said to have boasted of their exploits while imbibing vast quantities of imported wine - which they strained through their flowing moustaches! Their womenfolk were admired for their beauty; but the warriors seemed to pay them little attention, preferring the company of other men.

This characterisation was only a partial truth, at best. Modern archaeological techniques, combined with language research and the study of Celtic folklore have helped to create a more balanced picture. The British Celts built up a flourishing two way trade with their Gaulish Belgic neighbours and, later, their Roman overlords. Not only wine but other luxury commodities were paid for with exports of copper, tin, lead, silver and gold: as well as salt, corn, cattle and hides, together with slaves (from intertribal raiding) and hounds.

At the beginning of the period, iron started to be used to replace bronze. Small scale smelting was widespread; using an admixture of carbon to produce a superior alloy.

The Celtic religion was based on the balance between male and female influences, personified by Dagda, the protector of the tribe and Morrigan, the symbol of fertility. The Romans identified five Celtic deities with their own Mercury, Minerva, Jupiter, Mars and Apollo; but there were many others. The horse was specially venerated. Epona was a horse goddess and a horse's jaw was found squeezed into the top of one of the pits on the bypass route, possibly

This horse's jaw was found jammed into the top of a former Iron Age storage pit, on the bypass route. 'Epona' was a Celtic horse goddess. Although storage pits became used for rubbish once they no longer could be used for keeping the grain fresh; the positioning of this object could have had a ritual significance.

indicating a ritual significance. In addition: stags, ravens, bulls and boars all had divine significance. The interpreters of religion were the Druids, who spent some twenty years in training. Their responsibilities went well beyond controlling the sacrifices and settling religious questions; for they also acted as judges in criminal cases and as arbiters in civil disputes. As the most educated element in Celtic society and guardians of the Celtic soul, their influence extended across the Channel to the tribes of northern Gaul. This brought them into increasing conflict with the expanding political power and cultural influences of Rome.

The social and agricultural sequence in the 'Knoyle' family community would have begun with the festival of 'Samain', which took place on the first of November.[10] This marked the end of the old year and the beginning of the new. Dagda and the female goddess Morrigan came together, which ensured fertility of the crops and tribal wellbeing during the year ahead. Within the family it was a time for merrymaking, to be enjoyed by all the family, especially the young women.

Christianity became adept at taking over pagan festivals and giving them a Christian significance, so 'Samain' has survived to this day as Hallowe'en.

As the daylight began to draw out, the Festival of 'Imbolc' was celebrated on the first of February. It seems to have been associated with Brigit, a celtic goddess of fertility, learning and healing. To the farming community it coincided with the beginning of the lambing season. The sheep were smaller than modern breeds, but closely akin to the surviving primitive breed of Soay sheep. These were probably domesticated in neolithic times and a number still exist on the small island of that name in the St. Kilda archipelago (they can also be found closer to home at the Cotswold Farm Park). Once again, this festival was Christianized, with Brigid, Abbess of Kildare c AD 525, being remembered on 1 February.

Soon it would be time to plough the ground ready for sowing the corn. The Celtic plough was an innovation of the Belgic tribes; being heavy and wooden with an iron tip; but with no means of turning the soil, which was merely scratched. The plough was pulled by two yoked oxen. These again were smaller than most modern breeds, similar to Dexters. Some improvement in the tilth could be gained by ploughing a second time at right angles. The two staple crops were: Spelt wheat (triticum spelta) and hulled six row barley (hardium polystichum); both sown with the seed broadcast by hand. In addition to grain; peas, beans and lentils were cultivated, while the produce of edible plants, fruits and berries supplemented the diet. Chicken farming was practised.[11] Horses were bred for war and for light draught work , though the harness used was poorly designed - so that the animal's strength could not be used to full effect. There were several varieties of domesticated dog; ranging in size from small pet breeds to large hunting dogs. Their skins would be removed from carcasses and the pelts put to use.

May Day has survived into modern consciousness. In its celtic form of 'Beltane', its agricultural significance was being the day on which Druids drove the cattle between two fires to protect them from disease. The feast was dedicated to Belenus (equated by the Romans to Mars) the God of War, but also honoured other goings out: to pasture, to hunt and to what the Encyclopaedia Britannica calls 'wooing'.

When the corn was ripe, it was cut with a hand sickle just below the ears; leaving most of the straw still in the ground. The ground was then grazed in turn by the cattle, sheep and finally the pigs - each of whom got benefit from the remnant, the pigs breaking up the soil as an added bonus. The corn would be threshed with hand flails and stored. Celebration of harvest home would centre on Mercury, the celtic god Lugh, who had his festival on the first of August.

The corn after threshing was stored in pits which had been very accurately dug using an iron mattock on a short handle. The pits could be up to about ten feet deep; beehive or bell shaped with very narrow mouths. As soon as the pit was filled with grain, it would be fitted with an airtight cover and sealed. Then the grain in contact with the damp pit sides would start to germinate and fungi to act upon it. The result was that the oxygen in the pit would soon be exhausted and replaced with carbon dioxide, which quickly brought the biological process to an end.[12] The corn would remain sound for up to a year. Once taken out, the partially germinated corn would be fed to the pigs and the pit walls burned to kill the bacteria. The pits would be usable

for a number of seasons, but eventually the burning would no longer be effective; at which point the pit would be reused for rubbish.

The top of one of the Iron Age storage pits on the bypass route. Bell or beehive shaped, the top would have been sealed with an airtight cover and the pit could be as much as ten feet deep.

The Romans

It was inevitable that what in the middle of the 1st century BC was fast becoming the most powerful nation in the then known world would in time affect the British Isles.

By the end of the 2nd century BC, Roman trade with southern Britain was flourishing, Hengistbury Head on the Dorset coast being a major trading port. Wine was shipped in slender pottery vessels (*amphorae*), along with figs, raw glass, metal vessels and a wide range of goods some of which were packed in pottery.

This purely peaceful contact was shattered by the ambition of Julius Caesar; who, in BC 59 was given command of the new and rebellious Celtic provinces in Gaul. Four years later, he was seeking a five year extension in office. He therefore wanted both to be able to present a spectacular success to the Roman people and to remind them of the dangers posed to them by the northern barbarians. Those very barbarians' ancestors had after all reached as far as the valley of the River Po in Northern Italy, just 50 years before.

An invasion of Britain seemed to fit the bill; so on August the 27th he struck across the Channel into Kent, with two legions under command – only to meet with unexpectedly fierce resistance. Although Caesar later tried to present the venture as just a late-season reconnaissance in force, it was in fact a rather botched affair. The Britons were indeed put to flight and sought a truce (which they soon broke); but they succeeded in ambushing the 7th Legion in September, using a highly mobile force including cavalry and chariots.

The invading fleet had been badly damaged in a Channel storm, while planned reinforcements had been forced to return to Gaul. So, after hastily repairing his ships, Caesar and his troops slipped back across the Channel under cover of darkness. Even this operation was fraught with difficulty, for the Morini tribe from the Boulogne area attacked the returning force as they disembarked.

Caesar quickly set the army to work preparing for a fresh assault in the spring of BC 54. In July, rather later than planned, he landed again in Kent. This time he had 800 ships, five legions and 2000 cavalry, with which he defeated a loose Celtic alliance under Cassivellaunus. He brutally laid waste large areas in the south-east. Then, aided by the treachery of the Trinovantes tribe from modern Essex, he stormed Cassivellaunus's stronghold in present-day Hertfordshire.

By now it was late in the campaigning season, the fleet had again suffered storm damage, opposition from the Britons was still fierce and there was serious unrest in Northern Gaul. Caesar therefore negotiated peace terms with Cassivellaunus, rewarded the treacherous Trinovantes with trading privileges and withdrew once more across the Channel.

Although the Durotriges of Dorset had not been directly involved, the effects of Caesar's incursion were far reaching. The tribes of the south-east became to some extent client states, merchant venturers from Rome expanded the trading links, and Roman culture and customs were increasingly felt. As one example, in 15 BC the powerful Atrebates tribal confederation on the Durotriges eastern border transformed their tribal stronghold at Silchester. Traditional round houses were superseded by rectangular Roman style buildings laid out on a grid of straight cobbled roads, later surrounded by massive defensive walls some of which are still visible today.

The Durotriges retained their organisation of tribal strongholds, but they did adopt their own coinage system for the first time. This was based on the gold 'stater' of Philip II of Macedon, who ruled from 359 to 356 BC.[1] On one side is a wreathed head of the god Apollo, and on the other a two-wheeled chariot pulled by a pair of prancing horses driven by a charioteer holding a whip. Philip's successors, Alexander the Great, Philip III and Cassander also issued the same coin. There were many Celtic mercenaries in the Macedonian armies. They were paid in staters, which they brought back to their homelands. Eventually these were adopted as currency by the Celts, who then began to issue their own coinage, copying the Macedonian design.

After Caesar's incursions, the south-eastern tribes started to issue coinage to their own design and to adopt Roman titles. Cymbeline for instance , whose Roman equivalent was Cunobelinus, added 'Rex' after his name on his coins. He remains a familiar figure, having been the subject of one of Shakespeare's plays, in which he is described as 'King of Britain'.

The Durotriges, however, were much less influenced by Roman ways. They stuck to a version of the Macedonian design, in which a laurel wreath predominated on one side, while a highly stylised horse and lots of chariot wheels adorned the other. At first, their coins contained about 80% silver with a little gold, but rapidly became debased, ending up at about the turn of the millennium as bronze with a silver wash or just plain bronze. The most likely reason for the debasement was that the Durotriges' trading links with

continental Europe became weaker; both because of the south-eastern tribes'
increasing closeness to Rome and because the tribe probably adopted an
anti-Roman policy to safeguard their independence. One good silver stater
and one bronze example have been found in Knoyle.

For nearly 90 years, the Romans left Britain in peace. They relied on
treaties with Cymbeline and Verica, ruler of the Atrebates of modern
Hampshire, Surrey and Sussex. Like Cymbeline, Verica also styled himself
'Rex'.

The first warning of change was a little farce played out by the 28 year
old Emperor Gaius (known as 'Caligula', literally 'little boot' – a nickname
given him by the troops from his habit of dressing in legionary uniform as a
child). Generally depicted, especially by his many enemies, as a mad tyrant;
he was certainly volatile, extremely cruel and intolerant of any criticism. In
the spring of AD 40, he decided to invade Britain. This was partly to recapture
the glory of Julius Caesar's campaign and possibly because he had been told
by an exiled British prince that the land was rich, and could be easily taken.
His troops were unenthusiastic, indeed close to mutiny – and may even have
refused to follow his ship as he embarked.

Disgusted at their conduct, or maybe just deranged, he ordered them
to fill their helmets with sea shells. These were then to be taken back to Rome
and a Triumph celebrated to commemorate the conquering of the ocean!

Soon afterwards, Rome had had enough. Just four months after his
return to the capital, Caligula was murdered along with his wife and daughter
by the Tribune of the Praetorian Guard, responsible for the Emperor's safety.

The chosen successor to Caligula was his uncle Claudius. Shambling,
physically unattractive and with coarse manners; on the day after the murder
he was discovered by the Praetorian Guard cowering in the palace.
Nevertheless, the troops proclaimed him Emperor and the Senate agreed.

Once in power, Claudius showed political skill, administrative ability
and an awareness of the need to keep the army happy. Above all, he had a
burning ambition to restore imperial credibility and popularity.

This last led him to seek to expand the frontiers of the Empire partly in
the south and east, but specifically by conquering Britain. This he saw as a
means of earning well deserved acclaim while putting an end to subversive
influences on Gaul, particularly from the British Druids.

To muster the necessary troops he uprooted four legions from their
permanent stations. Three of these were deployed on the Rhine, including
the II Legion Augusta. This was a highly unpopular move; for alongside the
regular troops were their camp followers, together with retired veterans who
had received grants of land nearby on completing their terms of service.

The Emperor first tried to calm the troops by sending his trusted former slave Narcissus to talk to them. This led to a riot; but the men returned to duty on learning that the loved and respected veteran Aulus Plautius was to be their field commander.

Claudius arranged that he himself should come across to Britain to assume command when conditions were favourable. That moment came as the army advanced on Camulodunum (Colchester). Claudius then arrived with reserves headed by the elite Praetorian Guard and a supply train including elephants.

The British chief Caratacus, a son of Cymbeline, was defeated and lost his capital, while the Southeastern tribes were subdued. Colchester was declared the centre of a new province with Aulus Plautius as Governor. With his British visit lasting just 16 days, Claudius then returned to Rome to celebrate a Triumph in great splendour.

The new Governor then set about his unfinished business. II Legion Augusta under the legate and future Emperor Vespasian was instructed to conquer the Durotriges of Dorset and the Belgae from the Somerset area.

Recent work[2] strongly indicates that the Second Legion did not actually arrive in Dorset until AD 44 or even AD 45. It was probably landed on the Hamworthy peninsula in Poole Harbour. A base was established at Lake Farm near Wimborne, which was garrisoned until the Legion's Headquarters moved to Exeter in about AD 61. With the Roman campaigning season limited to the summer months of April to September, the Legion seems to have camped during the winter in south-east Dorset and it was not until the third season that its task against the Durotriges was completed.

This operation took 13 battles and involved capturing 20 hill forts. In the Durotriges' area these included Badbury Rings, Hod Hill, South Cadbury and the great encampment at Maiden Castle just outside modern Dorchester. This vast earthwork, surrounded by entrenchments and ramparts stretching over 120 acres, was fiercely defended. Great stockpiles of carefully selected sling stones, each about half a pound (227 grams), were stored ready for use on sling platforms sited to protect against entry through the specially designed gateways.

The Romans employed sophisticated catapults known as 'ballistae', capable of despatching iron headed bolts which could wreak havoc among the defenders. Eventually, the Romans got close enough to engage in hand to hand fighting. The finding of a contemporary 'war cemetery' hurriedly dug has provided gruesome evidence of the ferocity of the struggle, with one ballista bolt having pierced right through a Briton's backbone.

The Roman victory, when it came, was decisive. Within two or three years at most, the rest of the tribal area was overcome, if not entirely pacified.

Queen Boudica (Boadicea) of the Iceni in Norfolk led a very serious revolt in AD 60; which was supported by at least a part of the Durotriges, for a fierce encounter with the Romans at South Cadbury left many Britons lying dead and unburied around the south-west gate. Once this revolt had been crushed with great severity, the local population settled down to three and a half centuries of Roman rule, most of it in peace and prosperity.

For them, the absence of tribal warfare and the adoption of Roman currency were the first obvious signs of change. Soon afterwards came the Roman surveyors and engineers building a military road from Poole to *Aquae Sulis* (Bath).

Military road building was an integral part of the Roman strategy. The engineers went to work close behind the advancing troops to consolidate control and support the forward elements. Thus, Lake became the centre of a road network linking it with Hod Hill (where there was a cavalry unit established within the former fort), Hamworthy, Badbury Rings, the new town of Dorchester, Old Sarum, Winchester and Wareham. Rapid construction was called for, so while standard methods were used on soft subsoils, the removal of topsoil was sometimes reckoned sufficient preparation to lay a bed of, say, flints on a harder surface such as chalk. As with parts of the road from Badbury Rings to Bath, the surface could be upgraded later, especially when required for civilian use.

Traces of this road from Badbury are clear as far north as neighbouring Semley, but then become uncertain. Indeed, some authorities have suggested that the Roman advance was so rapid that the route became obsolete for military purposes and was never completed throughout its whole length. However, the need to support military action with good communications and the finding of a significant number of coins within Knoyle close to the road line covering from the first to the fourth centuries argue otherwise.

One of the first to search for the road line systematically in East Knoyle by field walking and consulting both ancient and Ordnance Survey maps was the late G.B. Berry of Mere.[3] An employee of the Sun Insurance Company working in London he had a lively and enquiring mind. Although some of his alignments have been open to question, he had an eye for country, the ability to search diligently for clues and a real insight into Roman surveying concepts and methods.

Apart from the conclusions in Berry's book, what other evidence is there? The line of a lane in prolongation of the last certain point in Semley is straight in its northern section and leads towards 'The Street', the name given to a small portion of the North-South road through the historic centre of the village. 'Street' can indicate a connection with Roman roads although 'The Street' is found in a number of Wiltshire villages without such a link.

The line of flints marking the course of the Roman road from Badbury Rings to Bath appeared briefly during construction work on the bypass; exactly as predicted, in a northerly continuation of Leigh Lane.

More specifically, during the excavation of trenches for the village sewage system in 1972, a road buried four feet down was revealed. Mr Clifford Sully and his family inspected this by torchlight in heavy rain, as the trench was to be filled in first thing in the morning and the contractors would not wait. Measurements were taken and the road was found to be 17 feet wide and nine inches higher in the centre than at the edges. Construction was of stones similar to those quarried from Haddon Hill nearby; roughly three to four inches square and purpose laid. During the long drought of 1976, Mr Sully recorded numerous cropmarks about four feet wide further to the north-west.

Finally, one further piece of evidence came briefly to light during the construction of the village bypass in 1995. Precisely on the line of Leigh Lane, where the County Archaeological Officer had been alerted to the possibility of locating the Roman Road, a line of flints was exposed by the bulldozers. This was photographed that evening, just in time; for the next morning all traces were obliterated.

No Roman villa sites have so far been found in or near Knoyle.[4] This may simply be because they have not yet been discovered. Another possible explanation is that Knoyle may have been within a large imperial estate covering a wide expanse to the south-east of Bath, including both Salisbury Plain and Cranborne Chase. If so, it would probably have been run by slaves for the Emperor's benefit, with little or no surplus personal wealth reaching the inhabitants.

Even without a villa in the area displaying the new farming technology, changes would have been apparent. Ploughing was being made more efficient by the introduction of the coulter; an iron blade slicing into the ground in front of the ploughshare which turned the furrow.[5] The scythe became a two-handed tool and sickles were better balanced. The spring-handled shears still to be seen today were introduced, speeding up the task of sheep shearing.

More upland areas were taken into cultivation, though the clay soils in the lower southern part of the parish were still too heavy to come under the plough.

People's diet also improved in both variety and quality. Rye and oats were introduced: while cabbages, carrots, celery, parsnips, plums, mulberries and walnuts came onto the menu. A single venerable walnut tree survives in an old cider apple orchard close to the church. There are signs of a number of early dwellings there too – so perhaps one of the walnut's ancestors may have been planted by a Roman hand !

When the Romans invaded, the only native apple was *Malus sylvestris* (now very rare) which is bitter and practically inedible. Using grafting techniques learnt from the Greeks, they imported their own sweet varieties to start the process which, with careful cultivation and our temperate climate, have produced the superb range of English cooking, eating and cider apples which we enjoy (and sometimes neglect) today.

The sweet apple trail did not begin with the Romans. They thought that the fruit originated in Syria. However, research in molecular biology and a recent expedition to Kazakhstan in the former Soviet Union has shown that some survivors of the first known sweet apples are still to be found in the fragments of fruit forest remaining in the Tien-Shin mountain range. There they grow up to an altitude of over 5,000 feet enduring temperatures of 30C/86F in summer and -30C/-22F in the winter.[6]

In a rural settlement one would not expect to find identifiable remains of stone buildings. If there is a lack of verifiable evidence on how the Romano-

Britons lived in what is now Knoyle, there is an identified site of a Romano-British cemetery close to the probable line of the Roman road. There and nearby, coins have been found dating from the 1st to the late 4th Century.

Perhaps the finest is a silver *denarius* of the emperor Trajan (98-117); a successful general and a competent, honest administrator. Shortly before he died he declared his kinsman Hadrian his adopted son. Hadrian, as Emperor, ordered the building of the Wall that bears his name from the Solway to the Tyne during his inspection of Britain in AD 121.

Among the two dozen or so coins unearthed in the area of the cemetery were several others of special interest. One, dated between 222-235, has a very clear head of Julia Mamaea, the mother of the Emperor Severus Alexander. She displays a hairstyle that was to become very fashionable in the 1930s! There is a *follis* of Constantine the Great 307-337, who came to power in Britain following the death of his father in York, and later was responsible for the Roman Empire becoming a Christian institution – this coin was minted in London.

There are also coins of two usurping Emperors: The first was Postumus, who ruled in the West from 259 to 268. The second was the attractive character Carausius. He was appointed Commander of the British Fleet about AD 280, charged to clear the Channel of the seaborne pirates from northern Europe who were creating mayhem with shipping and communications. This he did with conspicuous success, becoming a popular hero. In 286 he established himself as an independent Emperor, with the next few years being both peaceful and prosperous. He improved the coinage, which had become very debased, displaying motifs depicting: 'Peace',' Happiness' and 'Rejoicing'. Often this sort of PR is just wish fulfilment, but here it seems to have been a genuine reflection of the state of the country. Sadly, in 293, Carausius was murdered by one of his team – Allectus – who reigned in his stead until Diocletian in Rome brought Britain back into the imperial fold. Government was reorganised, with *Britannia* divided into four (later five) provinces, Knoyle coming under Cirencester.

Finally, there is a very late 4th-century copper coin with the 'Chi-Rho' device demonstrating that Britain, like the rest of the Empire had become nominally Christian.

Shortly after the beginning of the 5th Century, coinage ceased to be supplied to Britain. In 406, the troops in Britain elected their own emperor, a man called Marcus; who was quickly followed by Gratian and finally Constantine III.

In 408 the Roman officials were ousted. In the same year a barbarian Saxon raid was repulsed, by which time the only imperial troops left in Britain

At top left is the earliest coin found in Knoyle: A Celtic silver-washed stater of the
Durotriges, dated to between BC 60 and AD 20. Next to it is a denarius of fine
silver. It is of the Roman Emperor Trajan, (AD 98-117) father of Hadrian who built
The Wall. Next again is a denarius dedicated to the Emperor's wife Julia Mamaea,
and dated AD 222-235. Although there is very little silver in this example (for the
debasement of the coinage was a recurring expedient when funds were short), the
hairstyle is well portrayed. It has a modern look, which would not have been out of
place in the 1920s. The last on the top line is a coin of AD 260-273, probably of
Galienus. It depicts 'Mars Pacifer' (Mars the bringer of Peace) and shows him with
helmet and wreath. On the bottom line a coin of the usurper Postumus AD 259-
268. This one shows 'Virtus' ('Courage') in full armour with spear and orb, it is
dated AD 261. The second in this row is a follis of Constantine the Great AD 307-
337, minted in London. A coin of Crispus Caesar from 317-326, also from London,
shows an altar with the legend 'Blessed Tranquillity'. Finally, a follis of Constantius I,
who campaigned in Britain and died at York, where Constantine was proclaimed
Emperor shortly afterwards. It demonstrates that Roman coinage was universal
throughout the Empire, for this coin was minted at Sisca in modern Croatia.

were probably the static frontier guard forces. By 410, the Romans had left.
Two years later the British Provincial Council appealed to the Emperor
Honorius, who told the province to look after its own defence. For a while,
coins continued in use in the towns, though often 'clipped' with slivers cut
from coin edges as the only source of silver available.

With the collapse of the currency, no formal central administration and
no one to whom to pay taxes or to provide services, the economic base was
destroyed. Knoyle, like the rest of the countryside, was reduced to a barter
economy. The Dark Ages had begun.

The Coming of the Saxons

The picture of life in what was soon to become Wessex after the departure of the Romans is like an old oil painting hanging above a cottage hearth; the details murky and indistinct.

No contemporary written accounts exist. The nearest in time is a tract by the monk Gildas, who was born in the late 400s.

His historical references are often suspect. They are, however, useful for comparison with documents said to have been collated in the ninth century by the Welshman Nennius. Finally, there is the Anglo-Saxon Chronicle, in which Bede (writing in the early 700s) made extensive use of Gildas' account.

Despite this, there are other references to Britain, place name studies and recent archaeological work; from which a pattern of life and events can be made out.

The threat to the local Britons was quite slow to materialise; with the Britons under their tribal leaders quite capable of united action when the threat became extreme. The Durotriges, centred on modern Dorset, were among those determined to defend their rich and relatively densely populated downland. They had the political will and organisational capacity to erect the massive Bokerly Dyke on their north-eastern boundary, still an impressive feature today.

The Saxon invaders were severely checked in about 486 at the Battle of Mount Badon. Exactly where this was remains uncertain, but it is likely to have been at Badbury Hill Camp, an early Iron Age site on the ridge west of Faringdon in Berkshire.

The leader of the Britons on this occasion is said to have been 'Arthur', the general commanding the troops of King Ambrosius Aurelianus. The Saxons were so demoralised by their defeat that many of them went back across the Channel and no further progress westward was made for a while.

This 'Arthur' may well have been the historical figure behind the wealth of Arthurian legends about King Arthur, Camelot and the Knights of the Round Table; later to be set in a mediaeval Age of Chivalry by Geoffrey of Monmouth.

At South Cadbury, some 20 miles west of Knoyle, recent finds of Dark Age pottery indicate that the old hillfort was reoccupied in the fifth century. In turn, this tends to support the local belief that the hillfort is identifiable with Camelot – the site even has an 'Arthur's Well'. Among local traditions is one which says that 'King Arthur and his men ride round the hills on horses shod with silver when there is a full moon'!

While Arthur may not have been the son of King Uther Pendragon and his Queen Ygierne – holding his sumptuous court at Cadbury/Camelot – he is likely to have been a historical leader killed in 539. This could have been at the Battle of Camlann, in which Arthur is said to have fought his son Mordred and both perished. Alternatively it may have happened in domestic or intertribal strife.

The name 'Camelot' seems to have no basis in historical fact. It was first used for Arthur's supposed capital by the French romancer Chretien de Troyes, writing in the 12th century – 'Camelot' being his corruption of the Roman name for Colchester. More significant is the discovery that in the centre of the defence works at Cadbury there once stood a great hall 60 feet by 30 feet; gabled at each end with a lofty thatched roof and low walls, probably of wattle and daub.[1]

Although victory at Mount Badon had secured some respite for the Britons, the Saxons landed near Calshot Castle in Hampshire in 495. The Jutes came ashore at Portsmouth in 501, and seven years later the British King Netonheaf was slain with 5,000 of his men near Netley.

Before long, the invaders surged up the Avon valley; only to be checked at Chalford south of Salisbury. The location of the British defences is preserved in the name 'Britford' a little to the north.

Within half a century, the Saxon and Jutish forces had broken out across Salisbury Plain. The Britons held on at Penselwood Ridge (still a Celtic-based place name) until being driven westward in 658; but the people of Knoyle almost certainly came under the Saxon yoke well before that.

The Saxons were chiefly valley dwellers at first. Archaeological finds and a burial ground suggest that a British settlement under Saxon control may have persisted on the higher ground. It has been suggested that the village name 'Clouds' in this area can be identified with the Celtic *clwyd* – a steep hillside. However, the more likely attribution is to Thomas Cloud, who was the landowner nearly a millennium later.

By about 700 Knoyle was becoming a Saxon group of settlements with its principal features well established over the next three and a half centuries. To the 'seeing eye' they are still there today.

To begin with, many parish place and field names have a Saxon ancestry. 'Knoyle' itself is generally reckoned to derive from *cnugel* – a knuckle – referring to the distinctive outline of the main hill, especially when viewed from the south.

'Breaches' means land newly taken into cultivation; 'Culverhayes' near The Green was a fenced in piece of land 'haeg' for wood pigeons, and there are at least six more 'hays' around the parish. 'Plashet' is a pond or shallow pool; 'Slades' a short valley and 'Steeple Close' has nothing to do with churches but is simply a steep wood.

The parish boundaries were largely fixed in Saxon times, with hints of an even earlier origin. In the second year after his election, the vigorous and able King Eadred (946-955) granted a land charter to his minister Aelfheah, assigning him 'ten hides at Cnugel'. Both this charter and one from King Eadwig (955-959) granting land to his 'faithful vassal Wiferth' in 956 spell out the boundary between East and West Knoyle in detail which can be traced today. In particular, there are references to 'The Old Dyke' defining its northern sector; which must mean that it existed in Romano-British times, if not earlier.[2]

A formal assembly point for the men of Knoyle and its tithings of Milton (meaning 'middle settlement', not 'mill') and Upton is suggested by the name 'Moot Field' – which the Ordnance Survey says has earthworks, though the traces are now slight. Here on high ground in the north of the parish, the men would have gathered one May morning in 878 to hear a proclamation from Alfred the Great; summoning them to join him just across the Blackmore Vale, where the 18th-century 'Alfred's Tower' now stands at the junction of the three counties of Wiltshire, Dorset and Somerset. Here the King mustered his forces before the Battle of Ethandun, at which he fell upon the Norsemen and gained a decisive victory. Some authorities place 'Ethandun' at Edington near Westbury citing follow up operations at Chippenham. Others locate the action at Edington on the low-lying Somerset poldens. In this latter setting, Stephen Scammell describes how the Norsemen were driven north-westward along a ridge between the marshes until penned up against the sea, where there is an earthwork still known as 'Danes' Camp'.[3] After a few days they surrendered unconditionally and, as both accounts agree, signed up to a peace treaty at Wedmore – less than a day's march from the Somerset site. Under that treaty, Alfred treated King Guthrum and his army generously, in that they were allowed to spend the winter at Cirencester before falling back into East Anglia. The King himself was baptised with Alfred as his sponsor, and most of his company followed suit. England was divided in two with Wessex firmly in Alfred's realm and the two rulers established a good working relationship.

It is tempting, but wrong, to regard the Dark Ages as those centuries in which all the village inhabitants eked out a living in a long drawn-out struggle of unrelieved squalor and wretchedness.

The legacy of Rome was certainly almost spent within a few decades: with communications decayed and centralised administration only slowly re-established. Indeed, recent research[4] suggests that 'By about AD 400 most of Britain was a wasteland of ruins and rubbish'. Throughout the period up to the Norman conquest, education was kept alive through the Church. As late as the latter part of the 8th century, it was a matter of note that the sovereign (King Alfred) could actually read and write. Texts were at first written only in Latin, using abbreviations usually only indicated by a line above the word – frustrating to decipher until the context is known, when like a good crossword the clues give up their secrets.

Although Christianity had become the official religion of the Roman Empire by the middle of the 4th century; by the time that Pope Gregory the Great sent Augustine into Kent in 597, he found Queen Bertha and her household the only baptised Christians around. After her husband Aethelbert had been baptised himself, the King ordered Augustine not only to build new churches but to repair existing ruins wherever he might please.[5]

While it is probably true that there was little active Christianity in the villages of rural Wessex, we cannot be quite sure of this. King Ine of the West Saxons, who reigned from 688 to 726, issued the earliest surviving law code for Wessex. In it he not only gave legal preference to the Anglo-Saxons over the Britons, some of whom must still have been identifiable, but also laid down rulings on Christian ceremonies.

One well documented and prominent Christian during this period was Aldhelm. Trained in Latin and Celtic Irish scholarship at Malmesbury Abbey by its Irish founder, he continued his studies at Canterbury. In about 675 he became Malmesbury's Abbot himself and in 705 was appointed first Bishop of the new diocese of Sherborne, with responsibility for Devon, Somerset, Dorset and Wiltshire.

The churchyard cross has been identified as being 9th- to 11th-century Saxon work. It may well have predated the first actual building on the site. The front is bowed, both sides are worked, but the back is not. This would support the view that it is in or close to its original position, being at the extreme west end of the churchyard.

The first church building is likely to have been a Saxon wooden structure, roofed with thatch.

Central or minster churches were established from which priests went out to serve the population over a wide area or *parochia* – the origin of the present day parish. Particular stress was laid on the importance of baptism, without which people were believed to be denied salvation.[6] An adult would gain through baptism new bonds of spiritual kinship; complementing the traditional framework of family bonding which Anglo-Saxons brought with them from the Continent.

There is just a hint that St. Mary's East Knoyle may have been one of these minster churches. In a recent book, historian and author Dr John Chandler suggests that the dedication of early churches 'may have something to tell us about Christian origins'. Although stressing that no chronological study or explanation has so far been attempted, he notes that in Wiltshire many of the probable minster churches bear a common dedication to St. Mary: Alderbury, Great Bedwyn, Bishop's Cannings, Calne, Cricklade, East Knoyle, Market Lavington, Marlborough, Potterne, Upavon and Wilton'.[7]

As laymen gradually came to accept the importance of baptism, parents would seek out a priest to christen their children, without waiting for the next regular visit. This became a matter of particular urgency if the child seemed sickly and likely to die.

In time it became clear that the far flung diocese of Sherborne was too cumbersome a unit to look after so wide an area. The monks of Sonning in Berkshire had established a religious house just over the Wiltshire boundary at Ramsbury. In 910 Ramsbury became the centre of a new diocese with responsibilities for Wiltshire, including East Knoyle. The Saxon bishops would now have been able to reorganise pastoral care on a more regular basis, leading in due course to the construction of permanent church buildings for parish use.

In East Knoyle the early churchyard cross still standing at the extreme west end of the churchyard could have been the first visible marker of Christian religious observance.[8] Crudely but robustly fashioned on three sides, with the fourth (west) side unworked, it may well be in or near its original position. There are some worn indentations on the convex front side which may be the remains of a decorative pattern.

Later, perhaps, a thatched rectangular wooden church may have been built, in turn giving way to the stone structure, whose characteristic blind arcading can be clearly seen on the outer North wall of the chancel. Estate churches, often adjoining the manor house, were the ancestor of the true parish church. In the reign of King Edward The Confessor (1042-66), there was a move towards building in stone, in a style often described as 'saxo-norman'. This was so called because it combines features of both Saxon and Norman architecture and thus it is difficult to say whether the work comes before the Norman conquest or after it. The arcading at St Mary's seems to fit into this mould.[9]

This 'saxo-norman' blind arcading is to be found on the North wall of the chancel. It is the oldest surviving part of the building.

There is no record of which priests were appointed to serve the parish until 1297, well after the Norman conquest – and, furthermore, the church is not mentioned in the Domesday Book. This latter omission does not mean that there was no church, but certainly indicates that it was not endowed with land, something which the Domesday Book assessors would have been sure to record.

Just five miles to the south, Alfred the Great founded Shaftesbury Abbey; destined to become one of the most magnificent in the land until its wanton destruction by Henry VIII. It is possible that the Abbey established a chapel, still in existence in 1610 in the area of Chapel Farm. If so, it may have predated the parish church. Its site is uncertain for it may now be buried among the farm's foundations, or it could have been in the corner of 'Chapel Field'. Until recently this had an extension on its southern edge, which might have accommodated a small building.

Ramsbury's time as a diocese was short, for it was absorbed by the diocese of Old Sarum in 1044 and there was no Bishop of Ramsbury for over 900 years. In the 1970s both the Ramsbury and Sherborne titles were revived and given to the two Suffragan (now 'Area') Bishops within the Diocese of Salisbury. Whether any of the Saxon bishops ever came to the village is unknown, but the modern Area Bishops have all been welcome visitors.

The first Saxon farmers arriving to settle would have found most of the existing cultivation on the higher ground where the soil was more easily worked. The newcomers were able to change this with the aid of the heavy Saxon plough; typically pulled by an 8-oxen team yoked in pairs. The heavy clay soils could now be tackled.

With scant reliable evidence available, it is difficult to set timescales over the 500-odd years of the Saxon period. It is clear, however, that Anglo-Saxon agriculture was a mix of crop and animal husbandry.[10]

Barley was by far the largest crop, used for brewing. Oats were sown in the spring for animal feed and porridge, with wheat and rye planted in the autumn. A wide range of fruits and vegetables was grown or harvested. None of these crops was new.

The growing of grass for hay and grazing was widespread. Wild animals were hunted and provided fresh meat in the winter: Red and roe deer, wild boar, wolf, bear and hare – though rabbits (and rats) were absent. Saxon farmers kept horses, cattle, sheep, goats, pigs (salted pork was a winter standby), poultry, dogs, cats and bees.

The honey produced was used as a general sweetener, but also as the main ingredient of mead. This alcoholic drink, fermented from honey and water was similar in style to that drunk by the Celts before them.[11] As celebrated in Saxon folklore, mead was the drink of the nobility: Kings and thanes.

The nobles were landowners, demanding various levels of service from their tenants and most of the rest of the population. In return, they could be called upon for military service, attending court, compulsory almsgiving and so on.[12]

The Church hierarchy extended from Bishops, Abbots and Abbesses down to novices; all subject to strict rules which determined every aspect of their lives.

Below the nobles were farmers, merchants and traders who could, if they prospered sufficiently, move into the nobility. In a rural settlement like East Knoyle, most people followed occupations to do with the land, such as ploughman, shepherd, swineherd, cowherd, cheesemaker, granary keeper and forester.

The carpenter was an important figure in the community, for wood was the most commonly used material. Although skills declined after the Roman era, a wide range of hand tools familiar today was in use.

At the bottom of the heap were the slaves. Some were born into serfdom, some were placed there as a punishment or having been captured in war. Some people even sold themselves into slavery. Although their quality of life could be very low, masters were able to free their slaves; either as a reward for faithful service given, or for the good of their own souls. There were only a handful of serfs in East Knoyle at the time of the Domesday survey (1086).

Weavers worked mainly with wool on an upright loom. While women's dress changed considerably during the period, men wore close fitting leggings and knee length tunics.[13] Although maybe few people in the village were wealthy, high class bronze and enamel brooches and other ornaments have been found in the parish.

The relative peace which enabled Wessex to prosper after Alfred's victory at Edington came under renewed threats from seaborne Danish raiders around the turn of the millennium. London succumbed to the Danish King Sweyn 'Forkbeard' in 1013, who became the ruler of all England. Edmund Ironside, who succeeded Sweyn, was himself defeated by Sweyn's son Canute – known to generations of schoolchildren for teaching his courtiers a lesson by sitting down on the Dorset seashore and forbidding the tide to come in. Canute died at Shaftesbury just five miles from Knoyle on 12 November 1035 aged about 40.

Originally a brutal rebel, Canute had brought peace and stability to England during his reign; which began to disintegrate after his death. Meanwhile, as Winston Churchill recalled 'across the waters of the English Channel a new military power was growing up. The Viking settlement founded in Normandy in the early years of the tenth century had become the most vigorous military state in France'. Over Wessex and all England a hurricane was soon to strike.

The Normans

Robert, sixth Duke of Normandy, looked out from his castle at Falaise on a tranquil scene: The town buildings clustered around the foot of the fortress for protection and the townspeople were going about their business in peace.

It had not always been so. The previous year his father had died and Robert's elder brother Richard had inherited the title. Robert, just 16 at the time, had rebelled against him, fortifying the town of Falaise as his base of operations. Richard besieged the castle, attacking it with all sorts of catapulted projectiles, including stones and rubbish carrying plague and fever germs.[1] Falaise surrendered. However, the sudden deaths of Richard and several of his companions shortly after they got back to Rouen was suspicious. Some thought that they had contracted the plague when laying siege to the castle, others suggested that they had been poisoned. Whatever the truth of the matter, Robert now had the title. It was, perhaps, an early instance of the skill and ruthlessness which was to earn him the double nicknames of 'The Magnificent' and 'The Devil'.

On this sunny evening, however, Robert was relaxing. As he gazed downward, his attention was caught by the stunningly beautiful young girl doing her family washing at the town spring. This was Arlette, the 15 year-old daughter of a rich tanner in the town.

Robert was smitten with love at first sight. He quickly established Arlette's identity, but held back from forcing the acquaintance too hastily. Instead, he spoke earnestly to her father. The tanner then approached her on Robert's behalf with an invitation to go and live with him at the castle. Arlette was intelligent and quite well educated. She was also what the Scots call 'canny' and modern city dwellers call 'streetwise'.

She replied gently and respectfully to her father. Still a virgin, she knew that love, not marriage, was the most that she could expect – also that her friends would probably be jealous. She agreed to go up to the castle on condition that she entered openly in daylight by the main gate, dressed in her most attractive gown, mounted on horseback and accompanied by her maid.

Robert was waiting to receive her. It seems that the attraction was mutual for their love grew to a rich maturity over the years. Well within a twelvemonth, a baby boy was born, to be called William. William the Bastard, who was not ashamed of his parentage, was to become Duke of Normandy and King of England too.

As was quite common in well-to-do families, the duty of providing 'mother's milk' was entrusted to a paid servant, rather than discharged by the natural mother. In William's case, he shared the wet nurse with another William: William FitzOsbern, son of the Seneschal (roughly 'High Steward') of Normandy. Thus began an enduring relationship of loyalty and friendship which lasted throughout their lives.

Fortunately for the Conqueror, FitzOsbern was both able and utterly trustworthy. He followed his father as Seneschal of Normandy in 1060 at the age of 32, and was awarded the lordship of Breteuil and its castle.[2] He married and there were three sons: Robert, the eldest, who sought a life in the church rather than in public life, William and Roger.

On his lands at Cormeilles, which was (and is) a pleasant market town in Normandy, he founded an abbey in 1055 which later contained his tomb and which survived until the French revolution.[3]

When the Conqueror decided on his invasion of England, FitzOsbern played a leading part in the preparations. He handed over his religious properties to the monks, took a co-ordinating role in the planning, and provided at his own expense 600 of the 700 men-of-war which assembled at Dives-sur-Mer and neighbouring ports. The ships then embarked nearly 14,000 men and after an enforced delay at Valery-sur-Somme made landfall at Pevensey in Sussex. Just three months after the critical battle at nearby Hastings, William was crowned King of England in Westminster Abbey on Christmas Day. His victorious campaign was virtually complete.

The Conqueror was very conscious of the value of the contribution made by his Norman subordinates and was generous in dividing the spoils of war. As his second-in-command FitzOsbern was created first Earl of Hereford, granted the strategically important Isle of Wight and, among other gifts, the lordship of the rich manor of Chenvil. 'Chenvil' seems to have been the best the Normans could do in getting their tongues round the Saxon name 'Cnugel'.

Very few of the manors remained in Saxon hands, and Knoyle was no exception. The person dispossessed was a lady, Aileva, who seems to have also had lands in the Chalke valley belonging to the Abbess of Wilton, and possibly another estate in Berkshire. According to the *Victoria County History*[4] Knoyle just before the Norman conquest was the largest single manor in the hands of a lay person, except for King Harold and members of his family.

It would be nice to think that FitzOsbern was able to relax in his manor of Knoyle, but it is doubtful if he would have had the time to do so. In the year

William FitzOsbern in his castle at Chepstow.

after the Battle of Hastings, he was put in charge of the army while the Conqueror was away, held the new castle of Norwich and undertook viceregal responsibilities in the North.

Also in 1067 he was sent to Chepstow in Monmouthshire to ensure the security both of the town and of the old Roman road leading into South Wales. To the north and east the town was protected by the River Wye, but the south and west lay open. He therefore ordered the building of a solid rampart to link the castle to the busy port; which was completed within five years. Rebuilt and enlarged in the 13th century and now a ruin, it remains an impressive structure on a superb site.

Not far away, on the other side of the River Severn at Shirehampton, monks who had accompanied FitzOsbern from Cormeilles built a priory in 1072 dedicated to the Virgin Mary. Nine centuries later, in the summer of 1971, Canon Evans and the Abbé Meron of Cormeilles met almost by chance in Chepstow. A warm relationship developed which led, in 1976, to the formal twinning of the two communities.

Early in 1071, FitzOsbern was sent back to Normandy to help Queen Matilda's nephew Beaudoin in a dispute over the Flemish succession. Accompanied by just ten knights, he was killed at the Battle of Cassel in Flanders on the 20th of February, still in his early forties.

In his will, Robert the monk (sworn to poverty as well as chastity and obedience) got nothing. William gained the titles, secular property and responsibilities in Normandy; while Roger became Earl of Hereford. Roger inherited FitzOsbern's English possessions including the manor of Chenvil/East Knoyle. Unfortunately, he does not seem to have inherited his father's sound political sense, for he was only able to enjoy his position for a few years.

In 1075, Ralph of Gael, Earl of Norfolk and Suffolk, married Roger's sister Emma. At the wedding feast, the two men planned a coup d'etat with Danish backing, at a time when the Conqueror was out of the country.[5] In the event, it all went badly wrong. Roger was contained in Herefordshire by loyal forces, Ralph lost a battle near Cambridge and fled to Brittany, while the promised Danish contingent arrived too late.

Roger lost all his possessions, including Knoyle, and was lucky to keep his head. Perhaps surprisingly, the Conqueror executed just one of the noblemen involved. This was the ill-starred Earl of Northumberland. He had married the King's niece, but she gave evidence against him. The Earl was sentenced to be beheaded on a hill outside Winchester; where the condemned man took so long to stumble through the Lord's Prayer that the executioner did not wait for him to finish.

Knoyle reverted to the King, who still held it when the Domesday survey was launched ten years later.

The coin on the left is rare. Found at Knoyle, it was minted at Winchester in William the Conqueror's reign. The other two are silver groats. The centre one, was minted in about 1422, just seven years after the Battle of Agincourt, was struck at Calais. The inner inscription confirms this: 'VILLA CALISIE'.

The late Stephen Scammell made a detailed study of Roman, Saxon and Norman units of measurement. He applied his findings both generally across the country and specifically to Knoyle.[6] By analysing the Domesday Book entries with his aid, a snapshot of the village comes to life. By a happy chance, two versions of the survey survive for Knoyle. The one most usually quoted is set out at Appendix 1. It is the final published version following the standard sequence adopted throughout the land. There is, however, an earlier draft of the return for the circuit which covered the counties of Devon, Cornwall, Somerset, Dorset and Wiltshire. This is known as the Exon Domesday and contains interesting extra detail.

As Sir Arthur Bryant has described him,[7] William was hard and ruthless, but 'above all, he was a merciless taxer,' his first act after his coronation on Christmas Day 1066 being to 'lay on a geld (tax) exceeding stiff'. In 1086, England was once more under the threat of a Danish invasion. In order to assess the financial resources available to counter it, the King sought accurate, detailed data in the following key areas: The ownership of each manor (both before the Conquest and in 1086); Parish dimensions, ploughing capacity, meadow, woodland, mills, fishponds and other productive resources.

In addition to recording the tenants-in chief, who held their lands directly from their sovereign, he wanted to learn about the sub-tenants, agricultural and other key workers. Churches were only to be mentioned if they held land. Finally, the surveyors were required to estimate overall values in pounds.

They went about their work by holding formal sessions in each county town, at which evidence was taken on oath. The counties were subdivided into 'hundreds': a Saxon term originally probably referring to the land needed to support a hundred peasant families. Knoyle at this time was part of Mere Hundred, though this was to change later. There was a long list of specific questions to be answered. The facts had to be supplied by the Sheriff (the King's officer), the Lords of the Manor, subtenants and representatives of each Hundred and of each village.

The two area measures used were the 'Ploughland' or 'carucate' (from the word *caruca* for the Saxon 8-oxen plough) and the 'Hide'. These Saxon units retained by their new Norman masters were not set areas but estimates of what the land could produce. The 'Ploughland' was the area that an ox-team could cultivate from seeding to harvest in a season; the 'Hide' was the matching taxation unit. Both were in fact logical concepts; being assessments of value obtainable. A ploughland might be about 40 acres, whereas rough pasture or woodland might be rated at one hide to 160 acres. The Normans took over the old Saxon register of hides which had been compiled many years before the conquest – indeed even before the struggle against the Danes in the early part of the 11th century. There had been many changes since then. Shaftesbury, as one example, despite its prestigious abbey, was no longer a prosperous borough. It had lost a third of its houses in the Danish wars and many were still in ruins in 1086.

Knoyle's People in 1086 and afterwards

Domesday Book Knoyle was not a single central settlement, but three: Knoyle, Milton (Middleton) and Upton. They were separate tithings within the same parish; with distinct identities which persist today.

It is doubtful whether any of the early Celtic settlements, based on inefficient ploughing of thin downland soils, survived into the Middle Ages. However, their Romano-British successors, working more substantial farms and using more advanced technology, may well have grown into the hamlets which acquired the Saxon names above. If one includes the enclosures or 'hays' (from the Saxon *hagh*) to be found in the south of the parish in 'Kinghay' and 'Friar's Hayes', the shape of today's village becomes recognisable in embryo. The spread of Anglo-Saxon field and place names listed in Appendix 2 at the end of this book gives support to this theory – as do coin finds, though few have been unearthed in the southern soils which have been much more disturbed over the last millennium.

The dominant outside influence in every village in England was that of King William, exercised though his county sheriff. This important official controlled the shire and the courts in each hundred as well as collecting the royal revenues. In the case of Knoyle, this was not always easy. The King's holding was exempt from paying geld tax, but the rest of the estate only paid up after much delay. The regime could be harsh and was bitterly resented by the Saxon people, who were left in no doubt that they were a conquered race. On the other hand, peace, order and the rule of law were strictly enforced, giving a security which had been lacking for many years.

The hundred had a court, meeting once a month and settling both criminal and civil cases according to traditional laws. Twice a year the Sheriff would preside himself.

At the apex of the social pyramid in the village itself was the Lord of the Manor. The first recorded holder of the office was the Saxon lady Aileva, then William FitzOsbern. He was followed by his rebellious son Roger whose lands were forfeited to the King. Shortly after the Domesday survey, in 1088, the King gave the Manor to the Earl of Warwick, whose family held it for the next hundred years.

Apart from the King, who held 17 ½ hides worth confiscated from Roger de Breteuil, both the Abbot of Glastonbury and the Abbess of Wilton had substantial holdings. Then there were three named tenants: Walter Giffard, Gilbert Maminot and Gozelin de Reveire – who sublet to a man called Saulf. Another Gilbert held land rated at one hide; which was probably a mixed smallholding of arable land cleared from the woods, with some meadow, pasture and woodland rights. Finally, there was the licensed huntsman Godric who held land rated at one 'virgate' i.e. a quarter of a hide and the tax unit for a yoke of two oxen.

Of the rest of the population, the most prosperous class were the 'villeins', followed by 'bordars', 'cotsetlers' or 'coscets', cottars – whose dwellings give us the modern word 'cottage', and lastly the serfs. The serfs worked the demesne land for the lord of the manor – 'demesne' being land kept in hand by the manor and not let out to tenants. The serfs, who numbered ten, would have been descendants of Romano-British captives taken by the Saxons during their campaigns of conquest. They had few rights, but could be set free and become *coliberti* – though still bound to their lord. The next chapter looks at how the various classes lived and worked together to make a community which grew steadily in prosperity until struck down by the Black Death.

The Village Community Takes Shape

When King William confiscated the manor from Roger de Breteuil, it became Knoyle Regis or King's Knoyle and stayed with that title when it was given to the Earl of Warwick. However, soon after the Bishop of Winchester bought the lordship from the Earl's descendants in the 1180s, it was renamed Knoyle Episcopi or Bishop's Knoyle (a title still used in some legal documents today). Apart from a hiccup during the Civil War, the Bishops retained the title until the 1870s, when it was assumed by the Ecclesiastical Commissioners. Their successors, the Church Commissioners, still assert that right in the 21st century. In the 14th century the parish, of which Hindon was then a part, was moved out of Mere Hundred. It became a detached part of Downton Hundred; which had been part of the Bishop's estate since the 7th century, along with Fonthill Bishop. This was, presumably, to make administration easier, which had been tightly controlled since at least the early 1300s.

The Villeins, who were freeborn, held land 'at the will of the lord and according to the custom of the manor'. At first this meant that the villein could be ejected at any time, but later the courts gave him some protection. They were also known as 'customary tenants' and their tenure was called 'copyhold', because the conditions of leasing were laid down and copied in the manor rolls. They were bound to offer regular services to the manor: perhaps three days a week on ploughing and sowing. They had to pay rent in cash and in kind as well, but might hold up to a hundred acres of land.

The Lord of the Manor was Chairman of the company, with his Steward as Managing Director. The Steward was Director of finance and responsible for discipline. The Bailiff kept a daily eye on all the lord's property, while the 'Reeve' was Chief Executive. He was elected each year from among the villeins; often by his fellows, but in some villages by the Lord of the Manor. He kept and submitted for audit all the accounts of income and expenditure on the manor farm – and had to pay for any shortfalls.

He was responsible for collecting the rents and customary payments to the lord. For his efforts he might be paid in various ways such as: receiving a

This magnificent fireplace, complete with its bread oven, dates from about 1300. It forms the East end of the former manor hall. Happily retained when the village hall was built in 1908, this part of the building is now generally known as 'The Billiard Room' because it was used as such between the two World Wars.

Lying next to the old boundaries of Park Coppice, which was the Bishop of Winchester's deer park, this building is reckoned to have been the deerkeeper's dwelling.

free allowance of wheat, having his own rent reduced, payment in cash, being allowed to graze animals on demesne lands and eating on occasion at the lord's table.

The next most important official was the Hayward. He was responsible for all crops from the time that they were sown. He supervised harvesting, storage and final distribution. His payment was similar to the Reeve's, but on a lower scale.

Below the villeins, but definitely inferior in status, were the Bordars. They would hold a cottage and a small parcel of land from the lord. This would often be 'bordland', on the fringe of the cultivated area. In return, they had to do menial jobs for the estate.

Even lower down, but still superior to the serfs, were the Cottars or Coscets. They also had a cottage from the lord; but they had an even heavier load of menial duties to perform.

One of the Bishop's more valuable possessions in the parish was his deer park – now Park Coppice and the Park Meads. Roe deer can still be seen there, whose ancestry might go back to 1263. In that year, Henry III gave his half brother the Bishop five bucks and fifteen does as a gift 'to stock his park at East Knoyle'.[1] While deer could enter the park quite freely, once inside they were kept in by a deer leap of a ditch and palings. This can still be traced behind the houses on the west side of The Street. On the edge of the park, in Church Road, is the thatched building which was most likely the dwelling and workshop of the Bishop's deer warden.

Quite distinct from the bishop's park, part of the land to the west of the Shaftesbury Road lay within the King's Forest of Gillingham, with its royal hunting lodge at King's Court, of which some earthworks remain. Until 1330, when part of it was 'disafforested', the whole was subject to Forest Law. This laid down savage penalties for poachers. Killing a deer could earn the death penalty, while just shooting at one could mean having your hands cut off, and for even disturbing one you could be blinded.[2] In later years, the milder punishment of fines became common. Privileges, such as that of 'pannage' –

allowing pigs into the forest especially during the time of the autumn acorn harvest, could be granted on payment.

Woodland generally, of which there was over 300 acres in Knoyle, was a most valuable resource. It provided timber for building, hazel for coppicing and making hurdles, feeding areas for pigs as mentioned above, and fuel for heating the houses.

There were about five acres of meadow. This was good land deliberately left unploughed and cut for hay. There were also over 600 acres of pasture.

The parish arable lands were worked on a primitive two field system, under which half was cultivated each year and the rest left lying fallow to recover. This was in contrast to many of the rich soils elsewhere in the county on which the more economical three field system of crop rotation was practised. There were separate field systems for Knoyle, Milton and Upton, reflecting the separate entities within the parish, which persist today. A water colour by

When Upton Manor was painted by Jane Bouverie of Knoyle House in 1868, it was known as 'The Priory', although this was never so. It had come down in the world by this time, being divided into three separate dwellings.

Jane Bouverie living at Knoyle House depicts the 16th-century Upton manor house under the title 'The Priory'. There is no evidence that it, or its site, was ever a working priory. However, it may well be the persistence of a folk memory, for land that later became the manor of Upton called 'Childecnoel' was sold from Gilbert de Breteuil's estate (probably the man named as holding land valued at one hide in Domesday Book). Michael, son of Reynold of Knoyle was the vendor and the Cistercian Abbey at Stanley, near Chippenham in north Wiltshire the buyer. They funded their purchase from a legacy of £20 bequeathed to them by St Hugh, Bishop of Lincoln. Three years later, they sold the property to Geoffrey de Lucy, Bishop of Winchester for the sum of £66 13s. 4d. in a deal which at a mark up of over 300% might make even 21st-century speculators blush! The Bishop gave it to the Prior and Convent of St. Swithin, only to take it back under a swapping arrangement with the Prior 80 years later. Like East Knoyle, the lordship of Upton manor now rests with the Church Commissioners.

Ploughing began as soon as the land was dry enough. This would have been earlier on the easily worked greensand than on the heavy clays. An eight-oxen team would manage to plough about an acre in a morning; but then had to be allowed to graze for the rest of the day.

The cereals sown were wheat, oats and barley. The tenants had to help cut and carry the corn at harvest time with specific targets set, being paid in cash and in kind. In Knoyle, each man had to reap an acre.

The major farming activity in the parish was sheep rearing. On all the Bishop's estates this was controlled by the stockkeeper; who oversaw flock management and organised exchanges and imports to improve quality.

At first, the sheep would most probably have been of the Wiltshire horn breed, once almost universal in the county. Both rams and ewes are horned and very light-fleeced. W.H. Hudson described the Wiltshire rather dismissively: 'Its head was big and clumsy, with a round nose, its legs were long and thick, its belly without wool . . . it was hard to fatten. On the other hand it was a sheep which had been from of old on the bare, open downs and was modified to suit the conditions, the scanty feed, the bleak, bare country and the long distances it had to travel to and from the pasture ground. It was a strong, healthy, intelligent animal.'[3]

When Hudson was writing on the shepherd's life at the beginning of the 20th century, the Wiltshire Horn had almost disappeared from the county. Happily, there is (in 2002) a fine flock in the neighbouring parish at Lower Pertwood.

The Bishop saw the need to improve the stock as early as 1208, when Lincolnshire rams were introduced. Just two years later, 882 fleeces of 'great wool' were produced on the East Knoyle manor lands. With a demesne flock of around a thousand sheep, there were probably three sheepfolds: for ewes, wethers (castrated rams) and yearlings. Sheep dung was valuable. Movable pens were shifted around using hurdles provided by the villeins as part of their manorial dues. The sheep were regularly weeded out, with unsuitable stock being fattened and sold for meat at Martinmas (November 11th). While much of the wool was sold and woven locally, some of the high quality fleeces

Wiltshire Horn rams from Mr Mark Houghton Brown's flock at Lower Pertwood,
looked after by his shepherd Mr Tim White. The un-horned animals are Lleyn
sheep from North Wales.

could have been exported, in which case Flanders would have been the most
likely destination – being the principal European cloth weaving centre.

The shepherd was an important man, freed from all other feudal duties.
He was a valued member of the manor's permanent staff; rewarded with a
mixture of allowances, special privileges, cash and payment in kind. His
position was, however, hard earned. Sheep could stray or be stolen. Some
would be taken by foxes – perhaps even by wolves in the early days, for they
were recorded in the King's Gillingham forest as late as 1220.

Lambing was an anxious time, then as now, but the remedies available
to treat ailments were very limited. Infectious disease could take a heavy toll,
though outbreaks were often confined to a small area. As one example, in
1235, which was a particularly bad year, only just over half of the lambs born
in Downton, Fonthill Bishop and East Knoyle survived.

The dreaded scourge of sheep scab struck the Knoyle flocks again and
again. At the end of the 13th century the mortality rate among lambs reached
almost 90%. The only treatment to hand was to anoint affected ewes with
sulphur.

As if all this were not enough, an unidentified disease known as *rubeus morbus* or 'bramble disease' attacked young stock, especially after shearing – causing many deaths. The *Victoria County History* quotes the former Director of a Veterinary Institution in India as suggesting that the disease was a form of skin anthrax, caused by primitive methods of shearing. Until the middle of the 14th century, the Bishop's farms used wine, copper (in the form of verdigris) and mercury to treat the outbreaks. After that tar and grease were used instead.

Cheesemaking was an expanding industry during this period. In the early 1200s, 400 to 500 cheeses would typically be produced by the parishes of Downton and Knoyle from the milk of a couple of dozen cows and several hundred ewes. By 1300, the volume had increased to between four and five hundred cheeses, produced at the rate of one to three a day between April and the end of September. A major cheese fair came to be held at Winchester in the latter part of October, before the onset of winter.

One activity that had existed since before the days of recorded history was the grinding of corn to make flour. The traditional way of doing this had progressed from pounding the corn in a shallow bowl to a workable family hand mill known as a 'quern'. However by the time of the Norman conquest it was becoming clear that with increasing yields, a more efficient means was required. Norman technology provided the answer and water-powered mills began to spread westwards across the country. The simple, robust device was made mainly of wood with a few iron parts, some stone and perhaps some brass. Water flowing under a wheel (an 'undershot wheel') used gearing to turn a movable upper millstone against a fixed lower one to expel ground corn at its edges.[4] The result was an enormous increase in milling capacity – and a profitable source of income for the lord of the manor once he could impose a ban on hand milling and create a monopoly.

Knoyle had no mill in 1086, for if it had this would certainly have been recorded and included in the tax evaluation. However, soon after 1200, there was a village water mill at Lushley in the west part of the parish near where several south-flowing streams come together. Unfortunately the name 'Lushley' occurs more than once in this area, and there is a 'Mill Mead' by Moor's Farm; so until or unless some archaeological traces can be found the exact location will remain uncertain. The Lugmarsh and Sqeak's Wood streams are both contenders for the site; bearing in mind that the water table was much higher in mediaeval times – so it takes a very wet winter to recreate a likely looking flow. The late Stephen Scammell identified an embankment on Gillingham Lane as the site of the mill dam.

It was not long before windmill technology had also appeared at Knoyle. The exact date is uncertain, but it must have been some while before 1377, because a new pair of sailyards were purchased in that year.[5] Its location is not proven either, but there is a clue in the round base on which the present tower mill may have been built in 1536.

The first windmill would have been a primitive but effective post mill. The central 'main post' was secured by ground stays, with crosstrees. These crosstrees would almost certainly have been buried in the ground to make the mill structure more stable. The main post allowed the mill structure, with its four sails and gearing to grind the millstones together, to be turned to face into the wind. This was done by means of a spar from the mill chamber; which could be secured in the desired position. Access to the mill chamber would have been by means of a ladder straddling the turning spar and leading to the rear of the mill, opposite the sails. The elevated plinth, on which the present tower mill stands, could have contained the turning circle.

As time went on, the tenant farmers gradually came to pay cash in lieu of performing actual feudal duties. They also began to lease manorial land on a regular annual basis or even for longer periods. They were able to build up substantial flocks of sheep on their own account and even to become landlords in a small way by subletting cottages held from the manor.

National events for the most part brushed lightly over the village, except when extra tithes were demanded to replenish the royal exchequer. However, the long drawn out struggle between King Stephen and the Empress Matilda who 'fought like dogs about a bone'[6] in the mid-12th century, disrupted the economy, impoverishing the country. Military expeditions, such as the crusades, might awaken religious or patriotic fervour, but the financial burden could be heavy. Unsuccessful campaigns often brought treaty payments in their wake. In 1189, Salisbury had to hand over the enormous sum of £25,000 for this purpose.

King John hosted hunting parties from his King's Court lodge at Gillingham, but his reluctant and bad tempered signing of Magna Carta in 1215 would have had little immediate impact. It was, after all, drafted to compel the king to acknowledge the privileged position of the barons and the church. With their status safeguarded, they would be more likely to agree to royal demands for more taxation. Some of the new freedoms gradually filtered down to the ordinary people. Above all, a universal system of royal justice was created, with judges visiting each county throughout the land and applying a standardised code of law. Principles were established which remain fundamental today.

A major change close at hand resulted from Bishop Poore's decision in 1217 to ask the Pope for permission to move his cathedral from its exposed and vulnerable position at Old Sarum. Having been Dean of the cathedral for 19 years, he knew well how draughty the hilltop site was, with the cathedral staff suffering terribly from severe rheumatism. Water was always short, the cathedral was in the line of fire from the castle, the soldiers behaved badly and interrupted services, and the wind was often such that 'the clerks can hardly hear one another sing'.[7] Relocation to a planned city at a riverside location , with a chequered street pattern still visible today, created a vibrant spiritual and commercial centre. This rapidly became, and remains, a magnet for the whole of South Wiltshire.

The estate's legal affairs were dealt with at twice yearly 'tourns' presided over by the Bishop's representative. Records were kept of dues or 'cert-money' paid as a licence for brewing, milling and butchery. Juries of freemen from the tithings of Knoyle and Milton might also occasionally present evidence of affrays and public nuisance, while failure to perform feudal duties could be examined and punished. The spring tourn took place at Hocktide, that is, the second Monday and Tuesday after Easter – a time of feasting and merrymaking. The autumn tourn was held at Martinmas (November 11th) coinciding with the pre-winter sheep sale.

So, what was 'The Nature of Knoyle' in 1348, after nearly three centuries of Norman rule? It was a stable community. There had been a definite, if not continuous, increase in prosperity over the period. The manor of Knoyle was run by an absentee landlord through his officials at central and village level, as a tightly controlled economic unit. There were separate systems of fields held in common with apportionments made for Knoyle, Milton, Upton, plus Hindon which was within the parish at this time. There was also an unusually high proportion of land held freehold; indeed some of the lowland farms had most probably been established on Knoyle Common as early as 1250. These were later to become Upper Leigh, Lower Leigh and Coleman's Farms and are still working 750 years later.

Sheep farming had greatly expanded. The lord's flock alone had been a thousand strong when he caused an estate survey to be made in 1208. During the next century and a half this figure often reached double that number, well above the average for the rest of his estate.

Within the village community, each section had little option but to conform to manorial demands. Those in specialist occupations had some job security, but strict obligations too. Ploughmen, for instance, were held closely responsible for the well-being of their valuable oxen. They bedded down alongside them at night. They were expected to encourage and motivate their charges at work, even by singing songs to them – something which the beasts apparently much appreciated.

Despite the general improvement in the quality of life, bad weather could wreak havoc on the grain harvests, with disastrous effect. Heavy summer rains in both 1315 and the following year brought severe flooding.[8] Only about a quarter of the grain crops could be harvested nation-wide. Prices rose more than fourfold in consequence, despite some attempt at control by central government. For those at the bottom of the social scale in particular, there was no way of affording even the basic necessities of life. Some people undoubtedly starved to death, while due to undernourishment many more fell an easy prey to diseases for which few remedies were available.

Even these recurring misfortunes paled into insignificance soon after two merchant ships – one of which was from Bristol – docked at Melcombe Regis (now the seafront hotel area of Weymouth) in June 1348. Along with the cargo of stores being unloaded there disembarked a sailor who had recently come from Gascony in France. He was carrying the deadly bubonic plague which had been spreading from Asia across Europe to the French channel ports. The Black Death, which was to change the face of every city, town and village throughout the land, had arrived.

The Black Death and its Aftermath

The Black Death or bubonic plague is a totally disgusting disease.[1] The bacillus is carried inside the stomach of fleas at one stage in its life cycle but becomes an often lethal infection when transferred to the bloodstream of rats – particularly the black rat. This unpleasant rodent, commonly found in ships, sewers and other insanitary conditions, was thus a carrier of pestilence to human beings.

The symptoms were easily recognisable. Although the lungs could be attacked – an assault that was almost always fatal – a rapidly swelling lump would typically appear under the armpit, or sometimes in the groin. If it grew and burst within a few days, there was a reasonable chance of survival. Otherwise, bleeding under the skin, unbearable pain, consuming thirst, nervous breakdown, insanity and death were the consequences; which no lancing or poulticing seemed able to avert.

In many Wiltshire villages, the death toll was up to fifty per cent. Knoyle was relatively fortunate to lose only about one third of its population. The reason why some communities either had fewer or less severe cases than others is unclear. Recent research by Dr Stephen O'Brien, Professors Jardine and Hart, Dr Titball and others centred upon an outbreak in 1665 in the village of Eyam in Derbyshire, with comparative data from across Europe.[2] Their findings suggest that the presence or absence of a gene known as Delta 32 may have been responsible – though if so, this poses almost as many questions as it answers.

Some attempts were made to succour the living and to combat the spread of infection. The Rector survived and it is to be hoped that he was among those who braved infection to provide comfort and to administer the last rites when necessary.

The importance of taking the dead away from the village was recognised. In Knoyle, there is a strong tradition that a plague pit was created within the bishop's wood of Park Coppice. Indeed the reputed open site, though peaceful today, has a certain sadness about it.

The Semley Plague Stone, used in the Great Plague of 1665. People from an infected village left money, sometimes dipped in vinegar, on a stone near the parish boundary. Food would be deposited there in return – to be collected. The Knoyle stone stood beyond Sheephouse Farm towards Hindon until about a century ago.

Plague-infected clothes were burnt. In this and in the later outbreaks which continued into the 17th century, a form of quarantine could be imposed. Plague stones were set up in remote spots at village boundaries. People within the village would leave money on them, perhaps previously washed in vinegar. In return food from neighbouring unaffected areas would be deposited for collection. The nearby village of Semley still has its plague stone, half way up the hill to Shaftesbury.[3] Knoyle's stone used to stand beyond Sheephouse Farm towards Hindon at a track junction; but it seems to have been removed and broken up about a hundred years ago.[4]

By 1349, when the village was beginning to recover from the ravages of the Plague, irreversible changes were taking place in village life, here as elsewhere. The Bishop of Winchester found that with less land in cultivation, the value of his estates had fallen and rents had to be reduced. Knoyle already had a relatively high acreage leased to tenants, and this increased. Landholding families were created who later began to climb the social scale.

While prices for farm produce generally fell, farm labourers became a scarce and sought-after commodity. They were able to demand and secure higher wages, and indeed to move elsewhere in search of better conditions. Landowners lamented these changes. They particularly resented the less servile, even arrogant attitude of their former economic dependants; but they were unable to restore the status quo in the face of the new market forces.

One bright spot for both bishop and villagers was the surging success of sheep farming. As the Plague receded, Knoyle sent lambs to restock depleted flocks across the Bishop's estates in Wiltshire. A ram and 64 ewes were also supplied to his manor at Rimpton in Somerset, which he used as a staging post for his important property at Taunton Deane.[5]

Over the next two centuries (East) Knoyle continued to develop and the lives of families and the individuals within them become easier to depict as more written records exist. The Rectors' names are known from 1297 onwards, but many other names begin to appear, not just the aristocracy and gentry, but ordinary people such as farmers, bailiffs, villagers who served on the manorial courts as jurors, tradesmen and many others.

The Goldsboroughs

One village family that eventually made social progress were the Goldsboroughs of Clouds and Upper Leigh.[6] Originating in the small Yorkshire village of Goldsborough near Knaresborough, one member of the family fought under Edward the Black Prince during his successful campaign in France around the time of the Battle of Poitiers in 1356. It is probable that he was rewarded with some land in Wiltshire, for during the next century Goldsboroughs became established as yeomen in Knoyle; sheep farmers and leaseholders from the Bishop of Winchester of the newly built windmill.

Over their first century here and more, the Goldsboroughs seem to have had the knack of getting into trouble with the authorities. In 1474, the Bishop's court fined Henry three pence (3d) for having taken toll for grinding corn and brewing contrary to 'the assize' – an order regulating the price of ale by its relation to the price of grain. John Goldsborough and others, 34 years later, were charged with pasturing 50 sheep over their permitted number on the common land. The defendants were ordered to rectify this by the time of the next court or to pay 11s. 4d. (57p) each – quite a considerable sum in those days.

Even then John's troubles were not over. He was sued by Richard Maynard over an unpaid debt of 6s. 8d. (33p) and fined 3d. (1p). He was also charged as a butcher selling meat outside the manor limits (thereby breaking his feudal contract with the lord of the manor) and again fined 3d. This sort of niggling offence seems to have gone on for the next 20 years.

In 1540 Robert Goldsborough married local girl Cicely, daughter of John and Lucy Hayter. Of their ten children, eight survived into adulthood. When he died at Upper Leigh farm, Robert left one shilling to Salisbury Cathedral, but two pounds each to East Knoyle church and the poor of the parish. To each of his daughters went £200, while the lease of the windmill was left to his widow. Son John got the household contents. Robert arranged to be buried under the north aisle of the church, for which he would have paid a handsome fee. This, together with the sizeable bequests he made, shows that despite his tangles with the law, his affairs must have prospered.

In 1589, a younger Robert was accused of being a papist (he was indeed an ardent Roman Catholic). Other charges included: bigamy with a second 'wife' whose identity was not specified; defacing the English bible which had been introduced into all churches – 'in three places in his own handwriting' and 'christening his children in corners'. It seems that both his marriage and the baptisms of his children had been performed in secret by a catholic priest instead of by the Rev. John Marvin, the Rector.

At last, the tide of the family troubles began to turn. Yet another Robert, eldest son of John and Joan, was baptised in the church in September 1574. In 1603 he married Mary, daughter of Thomas Benett of Pythouse, a definite step up the social ladder. By the time that Mary's younger children were being baptised a decade later, this Robert was being entered as 'Mr' in the parish register.

In 1625 he claimed the right to use a coat of arms. At first the heralds refused to recognise his claim. Later however, when he had paid appropriate fees, he was allowed to use the arms carried by the Yorkshire branch of the family. At

The reputed arms granted to the Goldsborough family of Knoyle: A silver cross on a blue background.

last, the Wiltshire Goldsboroughs had joined the ranks of the gentry.

In the Civil War, two Goldsboroughs were commissioned as Captains in the royalist cavalry. At least one of them survived until the restoration of the monarchy in 1660. There is a tablet to Mary Goldsborough in the church porch. She died on her 39th birthday in 1644. Her epitaph quotes *Ecclesiastes* Chapter 7 with more faith than most mortals can manage: 'The day of death is better than the day of one's birth'.

The family bought an early version of Clouds House in 1551 and Robert built a new house on the site, of which nothing now remains. Augustine sold the estate in 1658.

While the family had its colourful side, and Goldsboroughs were quite often defendants in the manorial courts as well as jurors, they stood firm for the crown and the constitution, produced clergymen, schoolmasters and medical men. Some of their kinsmen emigrated to America, becoming a well known and respected family in Maryland.[6]

So far as is known, the Wiltshire Goldsboroughs have died out. There was a member at the Phoenix Inn in Gillingham in 1875 and another lived in Mere in the early years of the 20th century.

Henry VIII, the Seymour Family and the Reformation

The Seymour family took its name from St. Maur in Normandy. They gained lands in Monmouthshire in the 13th century and in Somerset in the 14th. By the end of the next century, Sir John Seymour was Warden of Savernake Forest near Marlborough, having inherited the position through the Esturmy family. He lived at Wolf Hall near Burbage with his wife, where they brought up a family of ten children; the third of whom was Jane, described as 'a clever, cautious but unscrupulous girl'.[1]

Sir John had helped to quell a rebellion in Cornwall in 1497 and accompanied Henry VIII to France. He stood high in royal esteem. Through her father's influence, Jane was appointed a lady-in-waiting to Henry's first wife Catherine of Aragon, the widow of his brother Prince Arthur. She later held the same post with Catherine's successor, Anne Boleyn.

By 1535, Henry's second marriage was failing, and the King became attracted to Jane. He made a four day visit to Wolf Hall to court her, during which the rest of the Seymours, it is said,[2] had to decamp to the manor barn.

There is a village tradition that he also travelled across the county with Jane to her relations in Knoyle, who are said to have lived on the site of what was later to become Knoyle House. The accuracy of this has not, so far, been established; as no proof of a house being there at that time has come to light. He would not have been able to hunt in the former Royal Forest of Gillingham, for the palace at King's Court had become ruinous and been demolished after its last owner, Edward III's queen, Philippa died in 1369. However, it is possible that Henry and his entourage may have been entertained by a visit to the bull-baiting pits at the eastern end of the parish on Knoyle Ridge above Summerleaze.[3] The King is known to have had a bear-baiting ring built in London at Southwark.

Although willing to accept the King's advances, Jane was only prepared to be his wife, not his mistress as Anne had been before Henry's marriage to Catherine had been annulled. How far this influenced the decision to bring the

Queen to trial for alleged incest with her own brother and adultery with five others on questionable evidence is unclear. Whether the charges were true or not, her execution left the way clear for Henry and Jane's marriage, which took place immediately afterwards.

Three days after the birth of her son, the future King Edward VI, she was required to join in the christening celebrations, though exhausted from a difficult confinement. She died just over a week later at Hampton Court.

There is no tradition of further visits to Knoyle by Jane after her marriage, but the Knoyle branch of the Seymour family clearly valued their royal connections. Their coat of arms carries the royal augmentation in the first and third quarters: fleurs de lys and three lions, which can be seen both in the church and on the inn sign of the

Queen Jane Seymour, from an old print of Holbein's portrait

The Seymour family, whose head is the Duke of Somerset, has always been proud of its royal connection. In the first and fourth quarters the coat of arms displays the lions of England with the fleurs de lis of France, still claimed by Tudor monarchs. The last foothold on the continental mainland was not lost until 1558, the last year of the reign of Queen Mary Tudor ('Bloody Mary') (and even then the claim was not abandoned, heraldically at least). She said she would die 'with Calais on my heart'. In the other two quarters are the golden angel wings representing St. Maur, from whom the family name is derived. These are the arms of Henry Seymour, father of Alfred. He married Jane Hopkinson of Bath whose own family arms are shown on a small shield in the centre of the main one. For the heraldically minded, this is known as an 'inescutcheon of pretence' meaning that Henry married an heiress, whose father had a coat of arms.

Seymour Arms in The Street. When Knoyle House was rebuilt and enlarged in 1881, the gutter pipe heads were adorned with cast iron Tudor roses, some of which survived the house's destruction in 1954.

Perhaps the strongest link with the Tudor court was in the Knoyle House art collection. Among a number of paintings by Old Masters was a portrait of Catherine Parr, Henry's sixth and last Queen. She married Anne's brother Thomas, Lord Seymour of Sudeley, who held the post of Lord High Admiral, though destined to be beheaded in the end. His portrait, attributed to Hans Holbein the Younger, stood alongside another by the same artist of the boy King Edward VI. Pride of place, however, went to the full length portrait of the King, one of four surviving attributed to Holbein.

After the last Knoyle Seymour (also Jane) died in 1943, the collection was sold by Christie, Manson and Woods in London on 19 January 1945. Henry's portrait was bought by the Walker Gallery in Liverpool for £3,360. The sale catalogue supports the view that the painting was possibly by Holbein's own hand by reason of the portrait's long association with the Seymour family.[4]

The main hall of Knoyle House in 1882, immediately after rebuilding. The Holbein portrait of Henry VIII can be seen on the left beyond the fireplace.

The picture is currently (March 2002) undergoing restoration prior to being the focus for a major exhibition in Liverpool in January 2003.

The story of Henry's break with Rome leading to the English Reformation is a tale of high politics, low cunning, and genuine religious zeal – with more than a dash of bigotry. It is outside the scope of this book to examine the tangled threads; but the consequences directly affected every parish in the land.

The church building, which was to show visible evidence of the force of the Reformation, was much changed from the simple stone chancel built in the 11th Century. Its side windows had been replaced with deep cut narrow ones of Early English style. This was at about the same time as Bishop Poore was building his new cathedral at New Sarum (Salisbury) in the first half of the 13th century. The church nave, north and south transepts were added at about that time too.

On the outside wall of the north transept are two interesting carved heads. A knight in chain mail stares fixedly northwards; while his wife on the other side of the window has an expression which clearly reflects a very strong character!

A South porch was added around 1400, and at some time around 1450, when the Rev Stephen Morpath was Rector, the fine bell tower was built.

Inside, the ribs of the present ringing chamber rest on four carved heads. One represents a rather worried-looking king (after all, the Wars of the Roses were in progress, a pretty turbulent time), another his queen and a third probably the master mason in charge of the work. The fourth is almost a cartoon character with a broad grin and with his tongue sticking out.

When the tower was being repaired in the 1890s, much of the central rubble material behind the faced stones was dug out. This yielded large fragments of pillars, a Saxon and a Norman capital, mediaeval graffiti, a little cup and large chunks of shaped window stone.

These masonry pieces could well have been used for infilling the rubble instead of being discarded after the former east window was replaced with the present large five-light traceried one. As well as by its up to date tracery style, the window's age is indicated by the dress of two carved angels on the outside wall, perched above the point of the window arch.

The tower's gargoyles, though weatherworn, still have interesting expressions on their faces. Noah, clasping the dove which he released from the ark to search for land, is clearly visible by the outside of the handsome west window in perpendicular style.

As a final whimsical touch, the carver wedged a happy laughing man wearing a nightcap at the south-east corner of the tower.

No-one in Knoyle could have been unaware of the Reformation taking place. The dissolution of Shaftesbury Abbey in 1539, 'the most wealthy and important nunnery in the Middle Ages',[5] was a sadly memorable event. Despite being founded by Alfred the Great himself, this counted for nothing when the nuns were pensioned off and the stones torn down. The town and the neighbourhood suffered too; for pilgrims no longer brought their trade, while the sick, the poor and the old were deprived of aid. None of the dispossessed nuns of Shaftesbury had any connection with Knoyle. Margery Hunton, however, a member of the village gentry family at one time living in Upton Manor, was one of 33 nuns expelled from the abbey at Amesbury at the Dissolution, receiving a small pension and a one-off grant. She came to live in Knoyle.

A 'True Certificate' of 1545 signed by Robert Goldisbrough (sic) and William Smith, the churchwardens, states:

> Wee doe present upon our oathes that one Margery Hunton of the Abbey of Amesbury now died and deceased within the Parish of East Knoyle alias Knoyle Magna the 17th of March in the year above. Dame Margerie Hunton buried March 17th.

It is not recorded precisely where Dame Margerie spent her final years, but by 1545 it could have been at what was later to be called Lower Leigh farm. This property had formerly belonged to St. Catherine's Chantry at Compton Pauncefoot in Somerset. At the Dissolution it passed to the Crown, then to John Whitehorn and John Bailey and from them on to William Hunton.

Other changes rapidly became apparent. With the introduction of the first English Prayer Book in 1549, the services became more readily understandable to the ordinary people.

A less welcome development was the physical destruction of 'images' during the short reign of King Edward VI (1547-53). It was probably at this time that a statue of the patron saint (the Virgin Mary) was removed from the lower niche on the south side of the tower, while its companion, of an unknown identity, was taken from the upper niche, and presumably similarly smashed.

There is a modern mystery over a third statue: one representing the Trinity. An existing figure in the Victoria and Albert Museum in London indicates that it would have shown God the Father, robed and crowned. In front of the lower part of the body is a small figure of Christ on the Cross, wearing a loin cloth. Although the Holy Spirit is sometimes shown as a dove, it is not physically represented there.

The Knoyle statue is now only a fragment, but Christ can be clearly seen. The whole was probably broken up at the same time as the niche figures; but the fragment was walled into stonework on the south side of the nave.

This may have been simply because it was a useful chunk of stone, or someone – appalled at the vandalism – may have sought to preserve a trace of its existence.

This is a fragment of a statue of the Trinity, which was usually depicted as a large God the Father enfolding a small crucified Jesus, with the Holy Spirit not portrayed. Found in a pillar on the South side of the nave during the restoration of 1876, it was probably put there after the Reformation, when many statues were destroyed in a burst of misapplied religious fervour. This may have been done to preserve the remnant.

In 1876 the fragment came to light during church restoration; attracting interest from the architect in charge, Sir Arthur Blomfield. However, that did not save it from being slung into the rectory garden, where it lay until rediscovered by the Fison family when they bought the house from the church in the 1930s. They presented it to Salisbury Museum. From there it passed to the museum in Mere. In 1995, the museum curator, Dr David Longbourne, kindly arranged for its return to Knoyle, where it now rests.

During the reign of Queen Mary ('Bloody Mary' to her enemies), the church at Knoyle briefly reverted to Roman Catholicism. Its next trials would come with the onset of the Civil War.

The church today, showing the 15th-century East window with the Tudor angels above it.

The Wren Connection, Civil War and Monarchy Restored

Most people know that Sir Christopher Wren was the famous architect who rebuilt St. Paul's Cathedral after the Great Fire of London. Most Knoylians know that he was born in the village. If they forget, there is an inscribed stone plinth in the Square opposite the War Memorial to remind them.

Less well known is Sir Christopher's father, also called Christopher, Doctor of Divinity, Rector of East Knoyle, Dean of Windsor, and a distinguished man in his own right. Some of his genes must have been passed on to his celebrated son.

The Wren family were originally of Danish descent. One member fought in Palestine under Richard the Lionheart and others at one time lived in County Durham.

The Reverend Dr Christopher Wren was born in 1589, the younger son of Francis, a citizen and mercer of London. He was educated at Merchant Taylors School under Lancelot Andrews and at St. John's College Oxford. Like his brother, Matthew, he entered the church, following him as Registrar of the Order of the Garter. As Bishop of Ely, Matthew was a friend and loyal supporter of Archbishop Laud, which brought him nothing but grief. He was tried by the Puritans and sentenced to 18 years imprisonment in the Tower of London.

Dr Christopher was not forgotten by Andrews, who became Bishop of Winchester in 1619; for the next year he appointed Wren Rector of Fonthill Bishop, where he remained the incumbent for 18 years. In 1623 he met and married 21 year old Mary Cox, daughter of Robert, the local squire, at which time he was 34. The wedding was in September, but a month later, just as he was about to leave for London, he became ill, being confined to bed until the following February. At about this time he also received from Bishop Andrews the living of East (or Bishop's) Knoyle, confirming him as a member of the High Church, academic side of the Court circle.

Under the royal patronage of Charles I his career blossomed. In 1628 he was made Chaplain in Ordinary to the King. Eight years later he took over as Garter Registrar and was appointed Dean of Windsor and of Wolverhampton. In 1638 the King gave him the rich living of Haseley in Oxfordshire.

The Wrens produced a family of eleven children, but only one son survived. One of the daughters, Susan, married the Reverend William Holder, when he was Sub Dean of the Chapel Royal. She earned Charles I's gratitude when she cured him of a painful poisoned finger. Holder was elected a Fellow of his college, Pembroke, Cambridge in 1640 and received the living of Bletchington in Oxfordshire two years later.

Despite holding down several jobs at once, there is every indication that Dr Wren was a conscientious churchman, with a special affection for Knoyle. He was also a man of business, not afraid to stand up for his rights.

Knoyle Rectory, now Knoyle Place. The elegant Georgian portion on the right was built in 1799. Some mediaeval features remain in the range on the left. Until 1805, the public road ran along the side of the house, when agreement was given to bend the route round to the South.

As if this were not enough, Dr Wren is described as 'being well skilled in the mathematicks'. He is recorded as having made 'a contrivance of a very strong roof' for Knoyle church, and is credited with making a still existing plan of the church, not an easy task as so many of the rectangles did not have true right angles of 90 degrees. There is firm evidence of his skill in architectural design in that in 1634 he was commissioned by Charles I's Queen, Henrietta Maria, to design a building worth over £13,000, for which a detailed estimate was submitted on 15th May the next year.

Dr Wren's most abiding achievement, however, was his work in refashioning the interior of the chancel. As Rector in those days, he was responsible for the chancel, while the parish had to look after the rest. This meant that he had a more or less free hand, with none of the business of seeking the grant of a faculty from the Chancellor of the Diocese – which modern day ministers and their flocks have to contend with.

Looking East towards the altar, the Doctor began with the columns of the chancel arch, later to be swept away in an ill-considered restoration in 1845, which replaced them with a fake Norman monstrosity. On the columns he indulged his sense of humour with quirky little religious riddles in Latin (Canon Hobday's solution from the detail recorded in Colt Hoare's *Hundred of Mere*):

A E	'Sic praecis,	'So rule that you may do
SIC SIS	Sic procis'	good'
AM	'Ama	'Love (and)
A	Ora'	Pray'
ORA		

UNUM NECESSARIUM		'One thing is needful'
A	'A (Deo)Apta'	'Ask (God) for
PTA		what is
O		fitting'

Behind the chancel arch the Doctor commissioned his plasterer, Robert Brockway of Frome St. Quintin, to copy his drawing of the Ascension of Christ. Only Jesus' lower half was visible, going up into a cloud, with the Apostles looking on.

Other panels deal with: Biblical texts, Jacob's ladder, and Abraham's intended sacrifice of his son Isaac, reprieved by God at the last moment. There was, and is, a panel almost certainly showing the Doctor himself at prayer under a dove in flight, the familiar quotation, 'Oh that I had wings of a dove,' reinforced by the Greek words for 'wingless' and 'yonder'.

The chancel ceiling was covered with further plasterwork of cherubs, clouds and the like. Over the next two hundred years, these began to fall off. They were replaced entirely with the present wooden roof in 1876.

Although the clouds of civil war had not yet seriously begun to threaten, the Doctor had two niggling problems demanding his attention.

First were the troubles of his chaplain in nearby Hindon; a parliamentary borough returning two MPs, but with its church subordinate to Knoyle. Under an agreement sanctioned by King Edward VI, the Hindon inhabitants became

Governors of the Free Chapel of
Hindon, responsible for the Chaplain's
stipend, but still within Knoyle parish.

In about 1626 the Reverend
Samuel Yerworth had been appointed.
Having, apparently, no private means,
he struggled to get his stipend
increased as church land leases were
renewed. Having succeeded in raising
his pay from a meagre £9 to £16 and
then to £24 over nine years, the tenants
and Governors had had enough and
sought to get him out of office. They
secured a writ against him for good
behaviour, which Thomas Shergold,
the Constable, served on him in the
chapel, imprisoning him there for a
whole day and a night. At three in the
afternoon the Chaplain slipped out
into his house which stood in the
chapelyard – only to have his door
broken open by the Deputy Constable
and two others and to be dragged out
and arrested. His persecution
continued; but a petition from
Yerworth to the Archbishop of
Canterbury and a summons to the
Constables to appear with the

*Dr Wren's self portrait on his plasterwork
in the chancel. He is using the prayer
from Psalm 55 'Oh that I had wings of a
dove'. The dove flies above him. The
two Greek words are 'Apteros'
('Wingless') and 'Apoteros' ('Yonder'). It
is astonishing that the roundhead
soldiers who battered the picture of The
Ascension over the chancel arch left this
panel alone.*

Chaplain before the Court of High Commission in London brought high-
level official intervention, which seems to have ended the matter.

The Hindon people resented the Rectors of Knoyle having a degree of
authority over their church affairs – for instance, marriages could only be
performed in the mother church – so this may be why Dr Wren took no
formal recorded part in resolving Yerworth's difficulties. In any case he had
his own struggles with authority on the fraught subject of saltpetre.

As with many substantial households, Knoyle rectory had a dovecote.
The doves, some white descendants of which were still to be seen in the area
at least until recently, provided a welcome supply of fresh meat during the
winter. Their droppings were a valuable source of saltpetre, used in the
manufacture of gunpowder.

In 1636 the saltpetreman for the four counties of Wiltshire, Hampshire, Dorset and Somerset was Thomas Thornhill. His job was to dig out pigeonhouses and make saltpetre ashes into loads. The parish Constables could then be ordered to arrange carriage to a central collection point.

Times were hard, due to competition for the product from soap and potash makers. In November of that year Thomas Thornhill and his brother Peter had hunted 36 miles round with nothing to show for it, so there had been no work for them in five weeks.

To make matters worse for the brothers, they became embroiled in a dispute with Dr Wren. The basic facts were clear, but their interpretation anything but straightforward. According to the Thornhills, workmen digging out the pigeonhouse had noticed a flaw in one wall, and warned that the structure might topple and the diggers be blamed for it. Five months later, they said, 'a tremendous wind over all the country brot [sic] it down'.

The dovecote that caused Dr Wren so much trouble still stands today, with later additions.

According to the Rector, there had been two incidents of damage, the first by Thornhill's predecessor, one Helyar. At that time, careless digging had caused the stone structure, with walls 20 feet high, to be so shaken that the Rector had had to buttress the eastern wall. On the latter occasion, the foundation had been undermined and the north wall fell in. This had resulted in the loss of three breeding birds, 'the least of which never yielded fewer than

30-40 dozen'. The whole flock had forsaken the dovecote, and the Rector also felt he might be sued for dilapidations of the structure, which he was required by law to maintain in working order. He estimated that repairs would cost him £20 5s. (£20.25).

Because the Doctor was an Officer of the Order of the Garter, he was entitled to the immediate protection of the Sovereign. The Saltpetre Commissioners, who came under the Admiralty, were ordered to investigate and enforce any recompense due to the Doctor.

Although one might expect the Commissioners to find for a complainant with such powerful connections; the evidence shows that not only did Thornhill get a fair hearing, but that the Lords of the Admiralty sought and obtained detailed local evidence from witnesses in the village. Thornhill's own servant, Austin Golsberg, testified that he had told the workmen that they had dug too near the north side and that they were a foot under the foundations.

Before the Commissioners could come to a decision, Thornhill fled to France, followed by further accusations: that he had been selling saltpetre to the country's enemies in Dunkirk.

The Wrens' fifth child but first son was Christopher 'primus', to distinguish him from the architect. Born in 1631, he was barely alive when born. Dying 'within the hour', there was just time to baptise him before his brief life expired. He was buried on the west side of the north door within the chancel, though there is no visible memorial. An indication of the perils of childhood is that within even such a reasonably well-off family as the Wrens, there was a succession of tragedies. Before Christopher (primus) was born, Elizabeth, one year earlier, died within 12 hours because of (as the doctor recorded) 'the umbilicus being badly tied off by fault of the midwife, she lost all her blood and died within 12 hours'. Elizabeth (the 2nd), born in 1633, fell ill with 'phthisis' (specifically probably tuberculosis of the lung) and died after a year's illness; the 'said maid was of the most acute intelligence, singular modest and of purest morals'. Finally, Rachel, born in 1636, contracted the 'King's evil' (tuberculosis of the lymph glands) at the age of 12. Twice she recovered, but in 1650 the disease reappeared and proved fatal.

Christopher 'secundus' was born on 20th October 1632, just before 8 o'clock in the evening. Mary had been expecting to have the baby in the rectory. However, a fire forced the family to evacuate the house, so that Christopher was actually born a couple of days afterwards in the house on the Square which later became known as Haslam's shop. The building survived as a grocer and draper's shop until 1877 or 1878 – depending on which account one reads – when Alfred Seymour had it pulled down as a hazard to traffic. He probably had in mind the projected rebuilding and enlargement of

Knoyle House opposite the shop, which would commence in two or three years' time. Alfred did then rescue the mullioned window of the room in which Christopher had been born, placing it in his new mansion. Some 73 years later, Knoyle House was demolished in its turn. Unfortunately the demolishers in 1954 either forgot or did not care about the historical connection; so that link with the village's most famous son was lost.

The building, demolished by Alfred Seymour in the 1870s, where Sir Christopher Wren was born because of a fire in the rectory. It later became known as 'Haslam's Shop' after its tenant, who was a grocer and draper.

As a boy, Christopher suffered from poor health, causing particular concern both to his father and to his elder sister, Susan. He obviously grew out of it eventually, since he lived to be over 90. He made up for his physical weakness by studying hard under a private tutor. When the doctor became Dean of Windsor in 1635, young Christopher spent much of his time at the deanery, becoming friends with Charles I's children. At the age of nine, his health was reckoned to be sufficiently robust to send him as a boarder to Westminster School, under the stern care of Dr Busby, who like Dr Wren was an ardent royalist.

At thirteen, he gave evidence of remarkable educational attainment, with particular skill in astronomy, which remained a lifelong interest. As the Civil War developed, he was able to continue his general studies under his sister Susan's husband, the Reverend Holder at Bletchington, and his mathematical education in London with Dr Charles Scarburgh. His subsequent

career as mathematician, scientific inventor and astronomer was remarkable enough; but it is from the age of 37 after the Great Fire of London, when he finally concentrated on architecture, that his genius became fully apparent. His achievements remain a source of pride in the village. The 350th anniversary of his birth was marked in 1982 with a flower festival in the church, bellringing, a service of thanksgiving for his life conducted by the Bishop of Ramsbury and a commemorative first day postal cover.

East Knoyle's most famous son, Sir Christopher Wren.

The rectory at Knoyle remained his home until 1647. Although no buildings in the village were designed by him, he is credited as a young teenager with offering sound

East Knoyle's First Day Cover, honouring the 350th anniversary of Sir Christopher's birth.

architectural advice on the design of the kitchen ceiling in his father's mediaeval rectory. He held the lease of a small property in Knoyle until surrendering it in 1662, after which he had no further known connection with the village.

Civil War

However noble the motive for engaging in warfare, however glorious the outcome, there will always be grief and distress; not only for the casualties and their families, but also for the civilian community. Their property may be damaged, their cattle and produce seized by armies 'living off the land' – with or without payment.

In civil war, there is an added dimension. Neighbouring towns and villages may be set against each other, old friendships destroyed, households and families torn apart – with father and son even fighting against each other on occasion. Those who seek to remain neutral can be swept aside. As in all conflicts, some will join armies just to fill their stomachs, to exercise power by bullying bystanders and the vanquished, or in the hope of plunder and personal gain.

Reluctance to shed blood and notions of chivalry at the outset weaken as attitudes harden. Mutual respect diminishes. Isolated acts of wanton cruelty and destruction multiply, justified by religious or political bigotry. Events in and around Knoyle during the long struggle between King and Parliament reflected all of this.

A declining cloth industry in the county, rising food prices and a succession of poor harvests were making life harder.

Archbishop Laud, appointed to Canterbury in 1633, introduced high church reforms designed to emphasise the mysticism of the parish priest, with such measures as separating the communion table (still in the church, though not in its original position) from the congregation by communion rails. These changes sharpened resentment among the Puritans, who were concerned with 'true doctrine' derived from the Bible, 'pure worship' and self-discipline.

The 'Divine Right of Kings' asserted the right to rule with accountability to God alone. This clashed with Parliamentary reluctance to sanction the new taxes demanded by Charles I, who was no longer able to rely on his existing revenues. In 1642 the Civil War began – a conflict which nobody wanted and all hoped would soon be over, with both parties confident that the other side would quickly see sense. In south-west Wiltshire they were soon to learn differently.

The principal local families were Royalist in sympathy, for which several of them were to suffer later. One, however, was singled out for special Parliamentary attention at an early stage.

The Arundell family had been connected with (Old) Wardour Castle since 1547. Thomas Arundell, who inherited it in 1592, came to royal notice three years later. During a siege to wrest the river port of Gran in north-west Hungary from the Ottoman Empire, he distinguished himself by capturing the Turkish standard. As a reward, the Emperor Rudolph II made him a Count of the Holy Roman Empire. In 1605 King James I raised him to the English peerage as Baron Arundell of Wardour.

The second Baron, Thomas, a Roman Catholic in the family tradition, went off to fight for the King at the start of the War. On May the 2nd 1643, his 60 year old wife Blanche was startled to find Sir Edward Hungerford at the castle gate.

He had been campaigning in Somerset, but had just returned to Wiltshire at the head of 700 cavalry and infantry. He had decided to make his mark and enrich the Parliamentary coffers by seizing the houses and property of prominent Royalists in the county. He accordingly brought up a further 600 men under Colonel William Strode to set matters in hand. He began by demanding that rents due to local Royalists, including Dr Wren, be paid to him instead of to the landowners. Christopher Williams and Henry Marshman of Knoyle were caught in the net and had to pay £25. In his plan to make an example of Royalist gentry, Hungerford decided to make a beginning with Wardour.

Ranged against this array of 1300 men were just 25 soldiers, Blanche and a number of women and children from the family and servants. She bravely refused to surrender the castle. For five days Hungerford attacked it rather ineffectively with two small cannon; but then he had mines laid in a couple of vaults which ran underneath the building.

Damage from the resulting explosions, lack of sleep and threats to blast an entrance through the walls – while lobbing firebombs through the shattered windows – sapped the defenders' morale. The resident Roman Catholic chaplain was authorised to negotiate terms of surrender, which took effect on 8th May.

The combatants were not molested. It would be nice to record that the rest were set at liberty and the property respected. Regrettably, this was not so. The women and children were taken captive to Shaftesbury. Despite a personal appeal by Lord Arundell to Sir William Waller, the Parliamentary general, the latter were packed off to be taught Puritan ways in Essex. The estate was thoroughly pillaged, with much wanton destruction. Almost everything moveable was looted or sold, even the fish in the fishponds. Physical damage to the fabric was extensive, but – after a lot of thought – it was decided not to pull the castle down.

At this stage, a local lawyer turned soldier who was to forge strong links with Knoyle took a leading part in events. He was Edmund Ludlow, born at Maiden Bradley just seven miles from Knoyle, the son of the extreme anti-royalist MP for Wiltshire. He held similar political views.

After obtaining a Bachelor of Arts degree at Brasenose College Oxford and being admitted to the Inner Temple, he joined the Parliamentary army as a 25 year-old and fought with the bodyguard of the Earl of Essex at the battles of Worcester and Edgehill. Posted to command a troop of cavalry in Sir Edward Hungerford's Regiment, he was appointed Governor of Wardour Castle when the decision was taken to preserve it. The garrison comprised his cavalry troop and a company of infantry.

The second Lord Arundell, away fighting for the King, died of wounds shortly after his wife's heroic defence. His son Henry, now third Baron Arundell, mustered a force and himself laid siege to his own castle.

Ludlow was advised by family and friends not to try and hold out. Even Parliament authorised him to quit if he wished, after smashing the defences. He showed his mettle by refusing to surrender and laying in stores and provisions.

In December, the trial of strength began in earnest. By February, after a number of breaches had been made in the walls, Sir Ralph Hopton, the Royalist army commander, sent reinforcements to Arundell, including troops recently returned from quelling a rebellion in Ireland. Some of these caused serious trouble to their own side. As Ludlow later wrote in his memoirs: 'And some of the forces from Ireland landed in the West and marched as far as Hindon towards Wardour Castle in order to besiege it but being informed that the person they were to dispossess was a Protestant (Ludlow) and he into whose hands they were to put it a Papist (Arundell) they mutinied against their officers'.

During this period when the Royalists were in local control, Dr Wren from his Windsor deanery was determined to recover his dues. He got a warrant from Sir Ralph Hopton to commandeer the services of some of Colonel Barnes' soldiers from among the besiegers, who speedily collected outstanding rents from the Rector's tenants. Williams and Marshman complained, but their objections were cast aside, a circumstance which was to have consequences later.

Conditions inside the castle rapidly worsened. After one or two false starts, conditions for surrender were agreed. Accordingly the 75 remaining defenders laid down their arms on 18th March. Sadly, the victors did not keep their promises. Two soldiers were executed and the remainder sent as prisoners to Oxford. Ludlow himself was also detained at Oxford, but in comfortable circumstances and was soon released in an exchange of prisoners. This kindly treatment was in part due to Arundell's efforts, for which Ludlow was duly grateful. He returned the kindness by revealing where he had hidden the Arundell family plate after finding it in a cupboard.

Ludlow's subsequent career was a roller-coaster one: distinguished military activity, occasional reverses and turbulent politics. Elected an MP in 1646, he was one of the King's judges and signed his death warrant. He later became alarmed at Oliver Cromwell's dictatorship and after his death refused to support his son Richard (known as 'Tumbledown Dick') as Lord Protector. By now he had become MP for Hindon, which continued to return him at the restoration of Charles II in 1660, even though he dared not appear at the hustings in person. The new Parliament declared his election void and after hiding near Holborn he fled to Dieppe. Exiling himself to Vevey on the shores of Lake Geneva, he wrote his memoirs. In 1689 he made one attempt to return to England, but with the House of Commons seeking to arrest him he went back to Switzerland, where he died three years later at the age of about 75.

Ludlow's specific links with Knoyle became established after Parliament had decided that bishops were redundant. When the Bishop's Lordship of the Manor of Knoyle was put up for sale with that of Upton also within the parish Ludlow bought them for £4,668 on 22nd January 1650. It is said that 'the obtaining of this cost him the whole of his wife's fortune'! He took a 'hands-on' interest in his new acquisition; ensuring that the customary Court Baron of the Lord of the Manor continued to be held, under the chairmanship of the Steward. A record of 1658 shows that Dorothy Willoughby successfully got permission from William Coles to inherit as tenant her late husband John's holding in Milton, on payment of a fee of 13s. 6d. (67.5p). By 1661, the lordship of the manor had been restored to the Bishops of Winchester.

The War treated Dr Wren and his family harshly, though young Christopher was little affected. Early on, in October 1642, the doctor was at Windsor when one Captain Fogg arrived at his house with a troop of Parliamentary cavalry. Claiming to have a warrant from the King, he demanded the keys to St. George's Chapel within the castle. The Dean refused. Forcing open the doors with crowbars, the soldiers then carried off all the altar plate and jewels that they could find – though they missed some of the smaller items which the Doctor had prudently buried in his garden.

Not content with this, the intruders ransacked his home and carted off many of his personal belongings, taking even his harpsichord. They also took away the records of the Order of the Garter.

Young Christopher was safe enough at his boarding school. The Doctor realised that with Windsor now in the centre of a strongly pro-Parliament area, he could expect a recurrence of this sort of harassment if he remained there. As soon as his daughter Susan and William Holder were married, he shut up shop, gathered together his wife, his daughters and his new son-in-law and made for Bristol, which was now in Royalist hands. When Mrs Wren died there while giving birth to another daughter, son Christopher could not get down from London for the funeral.

King Charles' dashing young general, Prince Rupert, soon found himself and the city under siege. There was no realistic hope of relief, so in September 1645 the Prince surrendered the city to Sir Thomas Fairfax. During his time in Bristol Dr Wren had written to his Knoyle churchwarden, Randall Dominick, authorising him to destroy his plasterwork in the chancel if it gave any offence to the Parliamentarians. However, when he and his family got back to Knoyle from Bristol, it was still intact.

They had not been back long when there came news of another attack on the Deanery at Windsor. Councillor of State Cornelius Holland, who was later to frame the charges of treason on which the King would be indicted, brought soldiers to search the garden. There they found the buried treasure, which disappeared with the altar plate already stolen. However, in about 1648, when some of the looted articles were put up for sale, Dr Wren was able to buy back the Garter records and the equally precious harpsichord.

Soon afterwards, most likely when Sir James Long had been captured in Devizes, a Royalist troop of cavalry appeared in the village. They were probably fleeing from that debâcle; and after a brief skirmish with pursuing Roundheads withdrew through Friars Hayes to the south-west. There is an old property in that part of the village which would have been affected that may still echo to the sounds of that engagement. A sense of 'turmoil, horses, cavalry and Roundheads' has been reported there in recent times.

Returning to undisputable fact, it is recorded that having been baulked in their endeavour, the pursuers turned their attention to the church, where they came upon the Rector surveying the handiwork of his plastering contractor, Robert Brockway. Accusing him of creating idolatrous Papist works of art, they removed him by force, but later released him – though not before smashing the representation of Christ's body being taken up into the clouds, and knocking off the heads of the Apostles watching the Ascension. If the figures in the niches on the church tower had not been removed a century earlier at the Reformation, they almost certainly were taken down now. The niche figures have never been found. The Apostles' heads, all except three of them, were refashioned somewhat inexpertly by Rector Morgell's wife nearly two centuries later. Surprisingly, the kneeling figure next to the Ascension panel on the north Wall was left untouched, so that we still have the presumed portrait of the plasterwork's creator.

Apart from the two main bodies of combatants, there was a loose grouping of gentry and farmers in Dorset and south Wiltshire known as 'The Clubmen'. They banded together to protect themselves from the depradations of both Royalists and Roundheads, both equally careless or wanton in leaving a trail of rural destruction. In the disturbed circumstances of 1645, they decided on action in the autumn after the crops had been harvested, the so-called 'Club rising'. The Rector, who was by then nearly sixty, with almost three decades of service as a parish priest, might seem an unlikely recruit. However, the 'rising' was quickly put down, with any alleged involvement being used as a source of evidence in subsequent legal proceedings.

In this year, Parliament took steps to neutralise royalist disaffection by authorising 'Committees for Compounding', in effect to wipe the slate clean for those who admitted royalist sympathies but were not otherwise 'delinquent', usually on payment of a fine. Dr Wren 'compounded' for his rectory and was accordingly fined.

Two years later, in May 1647, the Doctor was hauled up again, having to appear before the South Wiltshire Committee meeting at Falstone in the house of Sir George Vaughan. This time he was tried for 'Heretical Practices' (i.e. in creating the supposedly 'superstitious pictures' in the chancel). The charge of 'Delinquency' was brought against him once more, this time with specific reference to the Clubmen. Evidence from accusers and supporters was taken on oath and recorded in detail, with some but not all the witnesses being Knoyle people.

Members of the Williams and Marshman families trotted out their story of being made to pay rents twice during the second siege of Wardour, which was true enough. More damagingly, Andrew Marshman testified to the existence of an 'association' or paper being put up in Knoyle church, calling for volunteers to take part in a project for capturing not only Wardour, but also Plymouth, Lyme Regis, Poole and Southampton – all at the time in Parliament's hands. The Doctor was said to have agreed with it. Indeed, when Mr Benett of Pyt House nearby came to Knoyle to rally support for action, the Doctor is said to have encouraged him and 'gone forth with a calyver on his shoulder'.

Richard Dew, Parish Clerk at the time, also spoke about 'The Association' being published. He seems, perhaps understandably, to have been keen to gain favour with the Parliamentary side. If so, he got his reward, for seven years later he applied for and obtained the new post of Registrar in 1654, licensed to record births and burials, for which he was able to claim a fee of four old pence (1.5p). When Henerie Ricketts was married to Jeane Skelton in 1655, the Registrar duly recorded it but the couple had to present themselves to a Justice of the Peace. Henerie had to declare: 'I Henerie Ricketts do here in the presence of God, the searcher of all hearts, take thee Jeane Skelton for my wedded wife and before these witnesses, promise unto thee a loving and faithful husband.' Jeane made a matching declaration, promising also to obey her husband. This was the only form of marriage ceremony permitted, while baptisms and burial services were banned.

It does seem that Richard did care for his parish, since in the turbulent times of 1646, he hid the church silver, according to tradition in a compartment under the altar table. Eleven years later, he restored to the care of the Churchwardens: 'one silver bowl, two small silver plates and two flagons'. On that occasion, the Churchwardens granted him back pay for his former service of 13s. 4d. (67p) and appointed him Clerk for the ensuing year. One of the plates, made in 1635, still belongs to the church and is in occasional use.

A lively account was also given of Dean Wren and a company of Royalists seeking accommodation at one of the village inns, where Wren and its Commander shared a room. In the morning as he lay in bed Wren is supposed to have said: 'Sir, all is well, there's no danger, for I left word with my wife that if there were she should send word over the grounds', though how the innkeeper was able to hear this was not clear.

The silver patten (communion plate) presented to the church in Dr Wren's time as Rector. The inscription reads: Ergo donum hoc, moriens pie, Generosus Augustinus Templo haec Mervinus reliquit 1637. This translates as: 'Augustine Mervin, gentleman, dying piously, accordingly left this gift to this church, 1637'.

Another disaffected tenant of the Doctor was accused of perjury by one of his neighbours. Adolphus Darknall said that not only had William Pavy, then complaining of harshness from the Doctor, acknowledged himself well treated by the Rector, but also that he personally knew nothing of any involvement by the Rector in 'the Clubb business'. Furthermore, when Sir Thomas Fairfax had sent letters out calling for the Clubmen to stop their agitation, The Rector had got Darknall to make copies and publish them. Similarly, the Doctor's former Churchwarden, the Randall Dominick mentioned above, backed him up and swore that on his advice no men from Knoyle joined the Clubmen.

Amid this welter of confusion, there was a surprising gesture of support from some influential members of the Parliamentary party. Writing from the Committee of Lords and Commons for Sequestrations (i.e. Taking possession of private property and holding it for the benefit of the State) to the Wiltshire Committee, they said:

> GENTLEMEN:- There are come to our sight severall orders of Parliament and other public certificates some of them attested by our Committee whereby it appeareth that Dr. Christ. Wrenn hath been much employed by this Parliament and hath suffered many violences and plunderings in the performance of those employments – And likewise he hath contributed very large sums to the service of the State and bin a paynefull labourer in the work of the Ministry about thiss thirty years all which doe justly induce us to believe he is a Parson farr from meriting the Doome of sequestracion the punishment of most Malignant Ministers – wherefore we desire you to take into your serious consideracion and narrowly weigh the number and the quality of the witnesses and Informers, looking upon him with such favourable inclinacions as the due consideracion of the premisses do warrant, and what tenderness you please to afford him shall be esteemed an obligacion upon your very assured friends.
>
> John Danvers (like Ludlow, a regicide), Jas Herbert, Wm Stephens, J Evelyn(the diarist), W Lester

This was a pretty strongly worded appeal, but it was not enough. His Rectory was seized, he lost his job, and as the Falstone Day Book recorded under August 1647 a further fine was levied upon him: 'Christopher Wren DD being brought before us, additions to his present enlargement subscription £40'.

There is a village tradition that the Doctor remained in Knoyle for a further five years, working as a teacher, but the available evidence is against it. Almost certainly, he went to his son-in-law's parish of Bletchington, where he spent a peaceful retirement until his death in 1656.

Dr Wren's was not the only family to attract the attention of the Sequestrators. Those who were investigated included: John Fricker, holder of land from Lord Cottington; Augustine Gouldsberg; Matthew Mervyn of Upton Manor and Pertwood; Sir Roger Palmer, owner of 'Knoyle Farm' (location uncertain); Francis Toope, owner of 'Tucker's House' and Upper Leigh Farm; as well as the Willoughby family of West and East Knoyle.

As for the poor, their life was harder than usual, even though better-off parishioners regularly made donations to the parish overseers of the poor to relieve their distress. The administration of the Poor Laws had become relatively efficient and humane in the early years of Charles I's reign, more so than was to be the case later. Self-help was supplemented by the system of 'Briefs'. These were letters, published in the name of the King, calling for support for a wide range of good causes, local and national. Knoyle paid over the years for such causes as relief from flood, fire and tempest, persecuted Protestants abroad and the ransom of prisoners held by the Turks and 'other infidels'. Responsibility for gathering in the money was farmed out to contractors who often took some of the proceeds for themselves; but the actual collection was the Parish Clerk's responsibility. After the Brief had been read from the pulpit on a Sunday, he would stand at the church porch with his collecting bag and greet the departing congregation with 'Please remember the Brief!'.

The Knoyle poor benefited from this system in 1650. The Quarter Sessions in Salisbury made an order on 15th January as follows:

> Forasmuch as it appeareth to this Court that the parish of East Knoyle . . . is much depressed and charged with poore people and that there are very few poore people in Chilmarke in the same County. It is therefore thought fit and ordered by the Court that Chilmarke inhabitants shall contribute to the relieff [sic] of the parish of East Knoyle the sum of five shillings (25p) for the space of one month and afterwards two shillings and sixpence (12.5p) per week until the Court shall see cause to alter the same . . .

Any failure to pay up was to be referred to the Justices of the Peace to enforce compliance. Chilmark protested lustily that if the order was continued, the parish would have to turn their own poor out 'to wander up and down the country as others do'. The order was reduced to one shilling (5p) a week.

Parliament's replacement for Dr Wren at Knoyle was William Clifford. Not much is recorded about him except that he 'preacheth constantly twice every Lorde's daye'; though the parish administration seems to have been adequately maintained. When he died in 1655 he was succeeded by his son Samuel, who had previously been a minister in Somerset. Samuel was born in 1630 and educated at Frampton near Dorchester and in Salisbury. He obtained a Bachelor of Arts degree. He was known for his extraordinary memory and mastery of grammar. Although without doubt a Parliamentary sympathiser, he was prepared to disobey Parliament's decree if need be. He obviously felt that the wedding of his relation Elizabeth Clifford to John Sanger should be properly blessed and conducted a church marriage service himself. Their three children were also regularly baptised, the first in 1659, when the Act of Parliament forbidding this was still technically in force, though shortly to be repealed.

Restoration of the Monarchy

C harles II re-entered London on 29th May 1660, Oak Apple Day, to scenes of wild rejoicing. The people had had enough. Episcopal rule in the Church of England was re-established. The Bishop of Winchester issued an order 'silencing' Samuel Clifford on St. Bartholomew's Day (24th August). He was therefore ejected.

Samuel's successor Enoch Gray was also ejected, in favour of Dr Hawles, supported by his Curate, John Burgin; though both Mr Clifford and Mr Gray remained in the parish to care for nonconformists. There were 45 of them in 1676, including a small number of Baptists. Every now and then they were given a hard time. In 1683 Samuel Clifford, his wife, Richard Dew (described as schoolmaster) and the two constables for the parish all got into trouble for not attending at St. Mary's church. In the constables' case the Assizes ordered the steward of East Knoyle's second court, the court leet, to dismiss the two of them if they did not mend their ways.

William and Samuel Clifford and Enoch Gray were not mentioned in the framed list that hangs at the back of the church. In 1984, Richard Clifford, Secretary of the Clifford Association, brought this omission to notice. After some consideration, in 1990 the Parochial Church Council authorised an addition in the form of another smaller frame containing their three names; so the list is now complete.

When Charles II's illegitimate son the Duke of Monmouth landed at Lyme Regis to make his bid for the throne in 1685; there was much sympathy throughout Wessex, but the village as such was not apparently actively involved. This was probably because Monmouth withdrew westwards away from Wiltshire before his decisive defeat at the Battle of Sedgemoor in Somerset.

In 1688 James II retreated away from Salisbury. When William III landed at Torbay on 5th November, it took him a month to bring his army into Wiltshire, by which time his opponents had gone. Some Knoyle people would have seen him as he passed by through Hindon to Berwick St. Leonard, a mile or so to the East. At Berwick he stopped for the night as the guest of Mr Grobham Howes. From Berwick, he rode through Wilton to Salisbury on 4th December, leaving the county for Hungerford six days later. After over 50 years of struggle, the nation was now to have some peace.

Changing Times
The 18th Century

In our national life, great advances were made in the 18th century in science and technology, in music and in the arts. In the villages of Wessex, perhaps the greatest changes were in the way that land was used and in road communications.

The Enclosure Movement

It was now becoming widely recognised that the mediaeval common field system was no longer appropriate if the new, more efficient ways of farming were to be exploited.

When strips within a common field were replaced by larger compact areas, much higher yields could be achieved. Acts of Parliament and individual agreements were already being implemented in the parish by the start of the century – an indenture of 18th October 1679 records an agreement between two Knoyle farmers regarding land at Bath and Lugmarsh, both in the western part of the parish. They were now to become much more widespread, with the last major enclosure in the parish being at Summerleaze in the east in 1867. The enclosure agreement documents used to be kept in the oak Parish Chest, but can now be seen at the Wiltshire & Swindon Record Office in Trowbridge. The Parish Chest itself stood in the church until just a few years ago. One night thieves, stealing to order no doubt, broke in and removed it. Thus a part of the village heritage, with its five locks and dating from 1616, has been lost. The village's common land has not all disappeared; 88 acres still remain, gifted to the Parish Council for enjoyment and recreation some 30 years ago by the Lord of the Manor, the Church Commissioners.

Generally speaking, some effort was made to see that everyone got a fair deal, but there would always be winners and losers. At worst, the rich and powerful would acquire a nice, easily workable estate; while some on the margins might have to sell their portions and end up as landless labourers. Where a commoner lost the right to farm on the ancient common fields he or she would be given an allocation of land somewhere else in the parish. An example of this is the collection of small fields on the West side of the Shaftesbury road near to the Old Police House. These areas betray their origin by their name 'Allotments'. Schedules in the agreements would lay down the number of sheep which individual landholders might pasture on common land. Three landholders still have such specified rights on Haddon and elsewhere. The Milton common field which is now part of Milton Farm still showed the former strips until recently. In the south of the parish, the field near the former Turnpike on the west of the Shaftesbury Road, known as Great Ganns, had traces of mediaeval ridge and furrow cultivation still discernible until they were erased by modern ploughing methods.

A number of the old Saxon field names were still in use at this time, as they are today. These had been added to over the centuries, sometimes with descriptive titles, sometimes just to distinguish them for convenience, for instance 'Home Field', the one closest to the farmstead. With the break up of the common fields there came a need to identify who owned what.

Thus was built up a rich collection of several hundred field names in the parish. A catalogue of all known names, including those which have changed over time, is being prepared for the village archive, but it is a long job. A selection is given at Appendix 2.

Some names are self-explanatory, or yield their meaning with a little research. These include: 'Long Close', 'Turnip Ground', 'Four Acres', 'Great Ground', 'Picked Ground' and 'Picket Allotment' (both areas with sharp angles or corners), 'Breaches' (land recently taken into cultivation) and so on.

Some are named after their one-time owners: 'Perman's Ground' (the oldest decipherable tombstone in the churchyard commemorates a Perman who died in 1657), 'Dominick's Mead' (Randall Dominick was Dean Wren's churchwarden) and 'Parson's Ground' (a piece of glebe land).

'Skiddy Axe' is at the North end of Haddon Hill; where Knoyle roadbuilding stone used to be quarried (apparently with some difficulty!). 'Kite's Nest' on the Southern boundary is an interesting name, (no such birds there now). But what is one to make of 'The Drot', off White's Lane in Milton, or even 'Bunches', off Wise Lane? 'Bunches' may be a corruption of 'benches', alluding to the terracing formed by oxen ploughing, with turning circles at each end.

Drove Roads

The practice of driving sheep and cattle across Wessex from west to east is an ancient one. It goes back to at least 1312, when cattle were being sent from Wales into England for the King. It continued until the railways made droving over long distances uneconomic. Local movement continued well into the 20th Century.

The Welsh and westcountry farmers employed specialists to drive their stock to distant markets, to arrange their sale at auction and to bring the proceeds back. These men, and their assistants, were often rough characters, unable to read or write. However, they were very skilled at delivering their charges in good condition so as to fetch a good price. They were trusted to handle large sums of money.

The animals would typically be driven between ten and twelve miles in a day along broad drove roads between hedges 30 feet or more apart. Each evening the drover would arrange to turn his beasts into a farmer's field – for which he would pay cash. For his part, the farmer welcomed both the money and the manure. Once the animals were safely pastured, the drovers would adjourn to a local inn.

Cattle would be specially shod for the journey with 'cues' on each hoof. Oxen had to be shod on a wooden frame or 'thrown'. The shoeing nails would be kept in bacon fat, to prevent them going rusty, as this could cause gangrene. While old hands would know the routes from memory, Scots pines were often planted to act as markers which could be seen from a good distance.

One major route, known as the Western Drove Road, ran from Alfred's Tower, or possibly further to the west, to Fisherton Bridge in Salisbury. It passed over Charnage Down, by Willoughby Hedge, near Chicklade and Baverstock, then across south of Grovely Wood to Wilton. A number of milestones remain along the way, which Mr T. Morland identified as being of Bath stone about 3 foot 6 inches high (just over a metre), slightly tapering towards the top and with a distinctive arched head. As Morland has also pointed out, there is a further set of milestones between Amesbury and Mere, which can be confusing: but these are smaller with a round top and are of Chilmark stone.

When the turnpikes, discussed below, came into being they were to become hated by the drovers. They would go to great lengths to avoid paying the tolls on their beasts. In some places there would even be a parallel route, created just for the animal traffic.

The Ox Drove, which can be seen from where it leaves the A303 looping eastwards to the south of Chicklade, was convenient for Berwick Fair, held twice a year on Cold Berwick Hill to the north-east of Hindon. It is a spot where a number of local droves converge, including the West Knoyle Drove, also known as 'Monarch's Way', which can be traced running eastward from above Chapel Farm. Just beyond where it crosses the Shaftesbury–Warminster road (the A350), it is a textbook example of a drove road, with hedges 33 feet (10m) apart either side of a broad track. To see a drover's marker of Scots pines, it is only necessary to look at the clump near where the Willoughby Hedge–Hindon road crosses the A350.

The Berwick Fairs were held on 29th May and on 29th October, before the start of winter. The fair, though long discontinued, is still recalled in the paying of Knoyle's village charity, known as Berwick Fair Money. The off-duty drovers were spoilt for choice in seeking refreshment. In Hindon in 1754 there were over a dozen inns, now there are two. They also used to frequent the New Inn to the east of the fair, now the site of Chicklade Bottom Farm.

The Turnpike Roads

A t the start of the 17th century, England still largely relied on the decayed remains of the once superb Roman road system, supplemented by a web of local roads linking settlements and sometimes designed for packhorses. A number of them were probably in existence in prehistoric times, like the Great Ridgeway.

Each parish had to assume responsibility for highways within its boundaries, using 'Surveyors of the High Wayes' (paid £13 3s. 0d. in 1756) and 'Waymen' (paid £2 for 'picken of stones' two years earlier). Until 1691 the parishioners elected their own Surveyors, but after that the Justices of the Peace took responsibility, selecting them from a list provided by the parish Vestry. One such for 1824 survives, giving: 'a list of persons liable to serve the Office of Surveyor of the Highways for the tything of East Knoyle for the ensuing year'. Overseers of the Poor elected annually would provide labour for road work at desperately low rates of pay. As late as 1834 the Parish Vestry Meeting agreed that:

> . . . task work is preferable and we should adopt it where possible. We consider that in paying the labourer for wheeling stones the sum of three half pence (just over 0.5p) be paid the wheelbarrow to carry 1cwt. 2qrs.' (76kgs).

Even allowing for inflation, that is scarcely a princely sum.

While some of the parish officials tried to do a good job, they had little expertise. The result of their handiwork was often of little lasting use, becoming a source of fury to the entrepreneurs who were seeking to establish reliable, relatively fast road links between the growing centres of population and trade.

Under the concept of turnpikes, it was hoped to create through routes which would generate traffic on which tolls could be levied, providing a good rate of return to the investors. It was acknowledged that well constructed highways would bring great benefits to both the national and local economies. Each scheme required the approval of Parliament. From about 1750, this led to a quick succession of parliamentary bills being submitted by would-be road construction trusts for approval, employing the most modern techniques. Although John Macadam's method of creating an all-weather surface by using layers of small hard stones was not to be used until after the Napoleonic Wars in the next century, the new turnpikes were vastly better than anything which had been built for the last 1,300 years or so.

Travellers had to pause at each tollgate. After paying the appropriate fee, the turnpike keeper would allow the traffic to pass. Knoyle had two turnpikes passing through the village. The southern one had a brick built building on the west side of the Shaftesbury road, just about where the bypass and Holloway Lane meet. Traces of it came to light when the bypass was being built in 1995. This toll road was built in 1752. In 1829 the turnpike company was 'presented' (i.e. charged) at the Knoyle manorial court with encroaching on the parish waste to erect the building, but nothing much seems to have happened. In 1840 the gatekeeper was a 44-year-old lady called Ann Harding.

A separate trust undertook the building and operation of a direct route north to Warminster from the village. Previously, travellers had had to pass eastwards to Hindon before striking

A milestone on the Knoyle to Warminster turnpike, erected in 1767. The metal plate was added in 1840, but was stolen about 20 years ago. The stone itself nearly followed suit, but was discovered lying in the grass, abandoned either because it was too heavy or because the vandals were disturbed. It has now been secured by the County Council.

North. The Act authorising the building of this section was passed in 1765, and two years later the road was in use, complete with its milestones. One of these remains in the parish on the side of the former route of the A350, north of the crossing with the Willoughby Hedge–Hindon road (also turnpiked), with a gate at where that road joins the Amesbury–Mere road. An attempt was made to steal it when the raised section alongside was built, but fortunately the thieves failed to drag it away and it has now been secured. Its original inscription on the stone survives: 'Warminster VIII 1767'. In 1840, when a new Act of Parliament was passed for 'making and repairing several roads' in Warminster, an iron plate cast by Carson's Yard in Warminster was affixed, only to be stolen. So a piece of our history has been looted and is now probably displayed in someone's garden, with its context lost. Yet another of Carson's creations, a metal milepost, used to stand at the Upton turning, one mile south of the other. Small boys used to be able to hide in the back of it, but it has gone too, though another survives nearer Warminster.

Finally, there was the turnpike road from Willoughby Hedge running through to Fisherton Bridge in Salisbury. Milestone-hunters can find a good if slightly battered example just east of Sheephouse Farm. It is inscribed 'XVIII miles from Sarum 1766'.

The expansion of the rail network and the creation of a publicly funded road system sounded the death knell for the toll companies, which went into liquidation after years of falling revenues.

Village Charities

When Robert Compton and his wife Susanna held Chapel Farm from the Lord of the Manor, the state system for relieving distress among the poor was well established. An example was the system for employing the poor by rotation or what was commonly called 'going the rounds'. A later parish document of 1781 gives details of the sort of arrangements made:

> It were then agreed on that when any poor person could not get employment he shall apply to the overseer and he shall send him to be employed as follows: Every person who shall be taxed at ten pounds shall be obliged to employ such labourer one day, or pay him for one day. To every labourer having three children or more one shilling [5p] per day, having one or two children ten pence [4p].

The overseers of the poor, for the most part, tried to discharge their duties honestly. They were, however, under great pressure to keep the parish poor rate to the minimum level by ensuring that only those with a genuine claim were accepted as a charge on the ratepayers. Many needs of the poor were outside the system and so went unmet.

In his will of 1687, Robert Compton appointed his widow as sole executrix. After her death Chapel Farm was to go to Elizabeth Howe, daughter of Sir George Howe, Baronet, of Berwick St. Leonard. He made a number of specific bequests, but the then large sum of £300 was to be invested in land. The interest was to be used to bind out poor orphan children as apprentices and to 'relieving old poor people that are feeble and not able to earn a good maintenance' – and who were not getting support from the parish.

This was duly done, with a purchase also made by Mary Goldsbrough, of the former milling family, now on their way up the social scale. When Susanna put off her widow's weeds to marry Captain Arthur Fowke, the arrangements for relieving the poor were legally protected. Susanna herself bought a further 11 acres to add to the existing 27, while neighbours Francis Morley and Edward Sanger topped up Robert's gift with donations made to the Trustees.

When the Rector, the Reverend Charles Trippett, died in 1707, he left £100 to the Robert Compton Trustees. The interest was to be employed for a school for the poor children of the village. It paid the schoolmaster's salary, which was set at £5 a year. Finally, Mr Trippett's successor, Dr John Shaw, founded a charity in his will of 1742, with his widow Mary creating another in her own will.

These charities not only survive, but continue to meet a genuine need. Under a scheme agreed with the Charity Commission in 1975, the land purchased over two hundred years ago, together with investments in the Metropolitan Water Board and Equity Investment funds provided income of £1,749 in 2001. The Charity's fields are: Snook's Ground and Bleak Hill(to the north of Upton), Threshetts (west of Chapel Farm) and Poor Ground – this name refers to its status as Charity Land not to the quality of the field, which lies on the parish boundary to the west of Upton Farm.

There were 24 applications for assistance in 2001; most of them relating to the cost of domestic fuel. As well as providing emergency relief, in recent years help has been given to assist young people with educational costs and in starting up businesses.

The Trustees are, of course, entirely independent. However, it has been known for tenants of charity land to try to reduce their payments. In 1886, three years after Mr Percy Wyndham had completed the creation of a new Clouds House at a cost of £100,000, his tenants were struggling to cope with a slump in agriculture. In an approach to the Trustees he stated that he had been 'obliged to make large reductions to his tenants in the present state of agricultural matters'. Therefore, he claimed, the rent paid by him on his Charity Land should be reduced by 15%. The Trustees agreed. The same Percy Wyndham was a Trustee himself in 1897, when he resigned. In his place Charles Thomas Russell, the butler at Knoyle House, was appointed. 'Prospect House' had been built for him by Alfred Seymour in 1867. The property, with Russell's initials and the date 1867, stands on the east side of the Shaftesbury road.

Crime and Punishment

John Cross: First Fleeter

The Reverend Charles Wake put down his book and made his way across the rectory garden to the top end of the churchyard. One of his predecessors as Rector, Dean Wren (father of the architect), had cut steps down towards the back of the church tower over a century before.

It was time to christen John, youngest of the Cross family. The parents were waiting with some of the children in tow. No doubt, they thought, he would grow up to be a sturdy farm labourer like his father James.

John followed the family tradition and duly took up farm work – but in his case with a difference. Nearly twenty-seven years later, William Hacker and his son (also William), who were sheep farmers in nearby Semley, found that one of their more valuable animals had gone missing. They had seen John Cross, whom they knew slightly, hanging around with another younger man who turned out to be William Bartlett.

Sheep stealing was a serious matter; for since 1741 – when there had been a rash of such crimes across the country – it had become a capital offence. The magistrate at the preliminary hearing was William Burl(e)ton Doctor of Laws, a local man himself. Cross sought to implicate Bartlett as his accomplice, though how he thought that this would help him is not clear. Cross was committed for trial at Salisbury Assizes. Burlton was obviously less certain about Bartlett, who was detained 'for further examination on Tuesday next'.

They were confined in the gaol where the clock tower now stands close to the former Salisbury Infirmary, the spot marked by a relief carving of handcuffs and chains. Cross was formally charged with, 'stealing one wether sheep [a castrated ram] value 20 shillings (£1), the goods of William Hacker the elder,' on the sworn testimony of William and his son.

On Friday 11th February 1785, Bartlett was acquitted. On the same day Cross was found guilty as charged and sentenced to death by hanging. Despite or because of the severity of the law, judges were reluctant to impose

A clock tower now stands in Fisherton Street, Salisbury, where the gaol had been which held John Cross until he was transferred to the hulk 'Ceres' to await transportation to Australia. A plaque and this relief carving recall the earlier use of the site.

the full death penalty except in cases where the offence was an aggravated one. According to the *Sherborne Mercury* of 21st March, all those sentenced to hang were reprieved at the end of the Assizes session, before the justices left the city. Cross's amended sentence read: 'to be transported to the Eastern coast of New South Wales or some other of the islands adjacent as soon as conveniently may be, for and during the term of seven years'.

Held in Fisherton Anger gaol, Cross found himself not only alongside the others newly convicted, but also a further 22 with similar sentences. Most of the latter had been held for a year or more. The difficulty was that with the American colonies now independent, no arrangements had yet been made to transport prisoners to the newly agreed destination of New South Wales.

Cross was transferred from Fisherton to one of the notorious convict hulks – rotting old ships on the Thames. In his case it was the *Ceres* – an ironic name, since it refers to the Corn Goddess, or Goddess of Plenty.

From time to time the convicts were marched out to form working parties at Woolwich Arsenal; but for the most part they were kept huddled together in their rotting floating prison. It was perhaps some small consolation to them that those in the hulks seem to have been deemed to have started their sentences, while those ashore in gaols were not.

Most people either forgot or did not seem to care about these wretched people; but to its credit the *Salisbury & Winchester Journal* spoke up. Despite its rather laboured style of English, the paper's revulsion was genuine. Writing primarily of those still detained in local prisons, it argues:

> It is a heavy expense upon the county to maintain them so long after they ought to have been removed [no sympathy for the prisoners yet . . . but wait], but when it is considered that these poor wretches, whose crimes have driven them from society, and deprived them of every friend, are not only detained in cells, loaded with chains, for this long period, but that their sentences do not commence until they are actually transported or on board the hulks, humanity must recoil at the recital of so heavy an additional punishment, arising perhaps of the indolence of some servant of the state; nor is it thus with this prison alone, but generally and through the kingdom. Where is the patriotism, mercy and philanthropy of our men in power, if they can suffer such wanton cruelty as this to go unpunished? And above all what a reflection is it upon us as Englishmen, who boast our liberty above all other gifts, that by our indifference we tacitly approve of such enormity. To what purpose was the Act passed last session of Parliament for the transportation of felons?

Eventually, Cross and 200 or so other convicts were embarked in the large 445-ton chartered transport, the *Alexander* on the 6th January 1787. The charter contracts for the six transport ships had been drawn up with great care and in precise detail. They covered such things as: ventilation, medical arrangements (an approved surgeon to be on each ship), bedding, clothes, rations, exercise and so on – but the reality was less satisfactory.

On the positive side, the First Convict Fleet Commander, Captain Phillip RN was an able, humane and energetic man. He was assisted by Lieutenant Shortland RN, thoroughly experienced in transport and possessed of unusual zeal and energy in supervising arrangements across the whole fleet. Unfortunately, his powers were ill defined. Ships' masters (in our case Duncan Sinclair), surgeons (Balmain), and the Marine guard detachment Commanders (Lieutenant King) could and did squabble to the detriment of the prisoners.

The prisoners had arrived at Portsmouth ironed together with a guard of light cavalry. Embarkation took place in a season of severe gales. There was only a lax medical examination with many men already weak and suffering from contagious or infectious diseases.

There was then a two month delay, during which time the men were kept handcuffed together and eleven of Cross's companions died within a month. Lighters took some of the men off and the *Alexander* was thoroughly cleaned, smoked, sponged with tar and whitewashed. The prisoners began to

The ' Alexander', largest of the chartered transports in Captain Phillip's fleet and quite newly built. 16 convicts died, due to the insanitary conditions and the poor health of some of the men before they embarked. The fleet Commander's energetic action in cleansing and fumigating the ship prevented further lives being lost.

recover, but more died before sailing on 13th May, and on the first leg of the journey – to Tenerife.

After a long, arduous voyage via Rio de Janeiro, the Cape of Good Hope and Tasmania, all the fleet reached Botany Bay together on 20th January 1788, after a voyage of 251 days, with no ships lost – a great feat of navigation and seamanship.

One big complaint of Captain, now 'Governor' Phillip was that in selecting convicts for transportation, no thought had been given to choosing people with the skills needed to set a new colony on its feet.

Cross, however, was such a man with much needed agricultural skills. By 1790, he was working on James Furzer's farm. As the former First Lieutenant of Captain Phillip's flagship *HMS Sirius,* Furzer could probably take his pick. Indeed, it seems that Cross had responsibilities as a guard and was licensed to carry a firearm.

Three years later, the man from Knoyle set up house with fellow convict Elizabeth Davison and they raised a family of which at least four survived into adulthood. Once released, Cross became a significant landholder from grants and by purchase. He put his name to an address of thanks to Captain George Johnston of the New South Wales Corps, who had stood out against the tyrannical Governor Bligh; seemingly unable to learn restraint from his experience with *HMS Bounty.* Bligh was recalled to England.

Sadly, Cross began to face increasingly severe financial difficulties. By 1820, most of his land had been sold off by auction. He died on 27th December 1824, aged 68. His descendants multiplied, and now number over 3,000 in Australia. A well-researched and readable account of John Cross and Mary Davison's life together has been published by Lorraine Prothero, and a steady trickle of Cross's descendants visit St. Mary's church, East Knoyle, to record their names in the visitors' book.

James Wigmore: Murder Most Foul

The 1805 cheese-making season had just ended for the Wigmore family of (Upper) Leigh Farm, East Knoyle; with the last load being sent to Winchester's annual Cheese Fair, established in the reign of Queen Elizabeth I.

The head of the family was James Wigmore (senior), who was just a couple of years older than John Cross. He was well respected in the village, and had served as Deputy Overseer of the Poor in 1798, with responsibilities for the administration of Poor Relief in the village. He decided to ride across to the Fair, to check on prices, meet friends and to bring back the proceeds to the farm. He started back in the early evening of Wednesday 23rd October 1805. He had reached a point about a mile and a half from Stockbridge and just below Woolbury Ring, when he was accosted. The *Salisbury & Winchester Journal* reported on what is reckoned to have happened next:

It is supposed that he was stopped by footpads, and that on refusing to deliver his money, they fired at him, a ball having passed through his body, which, from its direction, was evidently fired by some person on foot. The body had lain some hours in the road, and was quite cold and stiff when discovered by a shepherd early in the morning. His horse was at a little distance in a field. The body was removed to Stockbridge, where an inquest was taken by the Coroner: – Verdict – 'Wilful murder by some person unknown'.

On the Saturday, the body was removed to Knoyle and buried the same day.

James left a widow, Jemima, and nine children aged between 8 and 23. The murdered man's great-grandson, writing to the rector 85 years later, recorded that James's widow 'lost her reason' on learning of her husband's death. She died almost exactly two years later. A flint cross used to mark the spot where the attack occurred, but was last seen in 1944. There is a story that a robber (whom some suspected of having been the murderer) was being transferred from Stockbridge to Winchester by horse and cart, when he escaped. It is said that an armed posse cornered him near Sandydown Farm, just east of Woolbury ring, and shot him dead.

If robbery was the motive for the murder, it failed in its object. Mr Wigmore's money and valuables were found untouched on his body.

The Death Knell

It probably was not a crime, but the circumstances were certainly bizarre. The *Salisbury and Winchester Journal* carried the following report on 23rd September 1799:

> On Friday Mr Whitmarsh took an inquest at East Knoyle on the body of Robert Elliot, a boy aged ten years, who was found hanged in one of the bell-ropes in the belfry adjoining the church. It is singular that a man was tolling the bell for a funeral at the time the accident happened, but he being a lunatic and dumb, it was impossible to get any information from him; and a man working in the church swore he did not cease tolling the knell a moment. Verdict: Accidental Death.

Robert was the eldest son of Charles Elliot and his wife Ann, who most probably lived in a cottage in Milton rented from the Seymour estate. He was buried in St. Mary's churchyard soon after the inquest closed.

Hard Times

The wars against Napoleon brought some famous British naval victories, but also great hardship on land. Britain had come to depend on a supply of corn from continental Europe. When this was cut off, English agricultural labourers in particular were quite unable to pay the high prices demanded for bread from their meagre wages.

The 17th-century saying that 'bread is the staff of life' applied almost 100% to many of the village labourers. Apart, perhaps, from milk, bread was only supplemented by tiny quantities of butter, cheese, bacon and tea. Fresh meat was very occasionally seen, though rabbits could be on the bill of fare.[1] The poorest families almost starved.

The magistrates at Speenhamland, near Newbury in the next door county of Berkshire, meeting at the *Pelican Inn*, devised a scheme to relieve distress which was soon adopted in Wiltshire and across the south of England. Rather than setting minimum wage levels, they decided to top them up from the parish rates. The value of the relief depended on the price of bread. Thus, each man was reckoned to need three gallon loaves (about eight and a half pounds) of bread a week, and wives and children a further one and a half loaves. The money then had to cover all other expenses.[2,3] The intention was good but the effect on small farmers who did not themselves hire labour was dire – for they had to pay to help their larger scale farming neighbours, with no benefit to themselves. Some contemporary critics condemned the system as encouraging the poor in idleness. In reality there were a number of employers who used it to lower wages and to put up rents, shrugging off their villainy by telling themselves that the parish would make up the difference.

This was, for those with the means to enjoy it, an age of elegance – but with 'its underlying poverty and degradation'.[4] Fine new mansions were given extensive parkland with sweeping views, but if those views were 'spoiled' by cottagers' dwellings, they might have to be removed. One quite local example is at Milton Abbas. There, the first earl of Dorchester removed the village from its original site between 1752 and 1787, but created a model settlement which is much visited by tourists. Mr Benett MP, of Pyt House, just over the parish boundary from Knoyle, pulled down cottages in front of his beautifully sited country house; an act still remembered with bitterness in 1965, 138 years later.[5]

Wellington's decisive victory at Waterloo on 18th June 1815 brought peace and national rejoicing. However, many local farmers who had grown corn to feed the nation – and to enjoy the high grain prices – now faced ruin, as European corn became widely available once more and prices fell sharply. Farming interests were well represented in Parliament and the Government was alarmed. The Corn Laws were quickly passed to keep out the cheap imported grain. Once again the plight of the poor went unheeded.

Agricultural wages in Wiltshire were some of the lowest in the country. Even though the price of necessities had dropped a little by 1821, smallpox stalked the land and a sheep disease ravaged the flocks.

With the excesses of the French revolution still fresh in people's minds, any form of social dissent from the lower orders was viewed with the deepest suspicion – and where possible actively discouraged. An East Knoyle vestry meeting in 1822 resolved that Mr R. Hurd, a printer in Shaftesbury, should be indicted for printing handbills calling for a meeting of labourers of the parish to resist the lowering of their wages from seven to six shillings (30p) a week. These people were about to feel the effects of what modern politicians have come to call a 'double whammy'. Many farm workers were not employed throughout the year; but were laid off from after harvest time until the spring. There was, however, some winter work to be had when the grain was to be threshed.

In barns like that of the Rector opposite the church, and across the parish, the grain would be threshed by men using hand flails. This implement was a heavy hinged stick which beat the opened sheaves of corn on the threshing floor, separating grain, chaff and straw. Typically, there would be double doors on opposite walls. This meant that the sheaves could be unloaded from carts on a drive through system. Both sets of doors could be opened during the operation to create a draught which blew away the chaff which would otherwise choke the lungs.[6]

This labour-intensive process fell an early victim to the industrial revolution. In the last years of the 18th century both steam and horse powered threshing machines were developed and brought into use, with one widely used local model being manufactured at the foundry in Salisbury.[7] The great advantage of the machines was not their efficiency, for the saving in cost on small farms was very little, but because they saved precious time in getting the product on to the market.

With go-ahead large landowners like John Benett of Pyt House setting the trend, the seeds of discontent were being sown. In Hampshire and Wiltshire

*A view up Church Road from Knoyle House, painted in 1845 by Jane Bouverie. At
left is an old cottage on the site of the War Memorial. It was once a dame's school.
The stocks outside have long since disappeared; though the equivalent ones in West
Knoyle, which were outside the church gate, lasted much longer. The gabled building
with a porch was the village school until the present building was opened in 1873.
Beyond the school is the tithe barn, burnt down in 1961. In 1845 the road ended at
the church. Part of the old manor house (by this time just the manor farm building)
can be seen across the line of the present road to Holloway which was driven through
in 1856. 'Bell Cottage', with its porch had yet to receive its fire warning bell.*

this was to burst forth after the harvest of 1830, with rick burning (which the
Wiltshire men did not support), forced levies of money and machine breaking.
Warnings were frequently sent under the signature of a mythical 'Captain
Swing', whose name became synonymous with the rising.

On the 25th November, the south-western corner of Wiltshire erupted,
with riots and machine breaking all around Knoyle to the east at Fonthill
Bishop, Fonthill Gifford, Tisbury and Tollard Royal. What were described as
'mobs' from Tisbury, Knoyle and Mere were reported to be poised to attack
machines in the Deverills to the north, but the major, and the most bloody
action, occurred on Mr Benett's property in 'The Battle of Pyt House'.

For some small-scale farmers, forced into using the machines against
their better judgement, their destruction was not too unwelcome, for it
prevented competitors from stealing a march on them. This, it has been
suggested, is why some farmers did not particularly resent their machines and

those of their neighbours being smashed, and had a fair measure of sympathy with the machine-breakers.[8]

The Battle of Pyt House, 25th November 1830

John Benett, owner of Pyt House and one of the County's MPs, took a direct personal interest in the management of his estate. As described earlier, he was not popular with some of his workers, while the Tory turned Radical commentator William Cobbett called him the 'gallon loaf man'. This was because in 1814, when giving evidence for Wiltshire magistrates, he stated that 'Every person in a labourer's family should have, per week, the price of a gallon loaf and three pence (3d, just 1.5p) over for feeding and clothing, exclusive of house rent, sickness and casual expenses'.[9]

At about 8 a.m. his bailiff, James Jay the younger, reported to him that a large body of men had assembled at Tisbury, three miles away. Mr Benett, with his steward Arthur Legg and Thomas Ball then rode out to Fonthill Gifford and confronted the crowd as they arrived.

Some of them had armed themselves with sticks, which they later supplemented with crowbars taken from a blacksmith's shop. The squire spoke to some of the men he knew to persuade them to disperse , without result. He then told them of a new proclamation which he had just brought down from London. In the name of the King it promised rewards of £50 (nearly three years' wages) for information leading to conviction of each machine breaker, with a free pardon if the informant were to be prosecuted himself. A reward of £500 was promised for conviction of arsonists, again with a free pardon for any informant except an actual perpetrator.[10]

The men vehemently denied any intention to burn property. They then split into three groups. One group broke into Mr Candy's farm to destroy a machine there, along with another which Mr Lampard had placed in a field nearby ready for them, presumably to avoid further damage. Lawn Farm was then attacked.

Squire Benett had particular reason to be worried, for he had two large machines himself. One was kept at Pyt House, worked by six horses, and parts of it were stored in a barn. The other was worked by water at the old watermill site on Lindley Farm nearby. He returned to Pyt House, soon followed by the rioters. Once again he tried to reason with them; combining his arguments with a refusal to consider increasing their wages and threats, reminding them of dire consequences if they broke his machines.

Thoroughly roused by now, the men did break into his barn; smashing his machine and pulling off the roof. Mr Benett sat on his horse and watched. After ten minutes or so, a silence fell on the crowd. Then a stone was thrown at the squire. It caught him between the eyes. His hat was knocked off, blood gushed from his nose and as his horse carried him out of range more stones were thrown, hitting his steward. The horse got tangled up with a team of Mr Benett's own cart horses, probably the one that had been used by John Brickell to draw up roadmaking stone from Lawn Quarry earlier that morning.

Their wrecking done, the men took no steps to approach Pyt House itself. Mr Benett had armed twenty of his own men who stood guard there while waiting for the Yeomanry to arrive. The Hindon Troop of the Wiltshire Yeomanry Cavalry had been summoned from their headquarters in Salisbury by a farmer from Hindon and had set out at 10.40 a.m. to reach the area. The men, meanwhile, made for Lindley Farm and smashed Mr Benett's water-powered machine. Afterwards, according to John Brickell, they broke open one of the bailiff's beer barrels and settled down to refresh themselves. The Hindon Troop, under their Captain, Mr William Wyndham of Dinton, and accompanied by Mr Wadham Wyndham, now arrived on the scene. They found the rioters in a cutting.

More stones were thrown by the men at this new enemy. The Riot Act was quickly read, the Troop divided into two sections and battle commenced – 44 yeomanry against several hundred rioters – cavalry sabres against sticks and iron bars. As John Brickell was to recall 53 years later:

> The cavalry did lay about them *wonderful* there – they slashed 'em about awful and one he were just agetting up into the wood when one of the cavalry did let off his horse pistol and shot 'im – the bullet did go in at back of his head and out t'other side – his name were John Harding.[11]

Mr Benett called upon Captain Wyndham not to allow any more shooting; but if John Brickell's account is accurate, it continued for some time until the rioters were surrounded.

Farm horses and carts were then hitched up, and 29 of the men were arrested and taken under escort to Salisbury. Some were put in the Infirmary, others in Fisherton Gaol. Brickell drove the first cart and 'the blood did trickle out of the waggons'. When the party reached the *Black Horse* at Chilmark (actually either the *Black Horse* at Teffont or the *Black Dog* at Chilmark):

> they did cry out for summat to drink, poor fellows, but the yeomanry wouldn't let them have nothing – they wouldn't. It were an awful cold night and they were most shrammed [frozen] with the frost.[12]

The dead man was a labourer from Tisbury, but according to Brickell his family lived 'up Knoyle' and 'they come and carried him home'. If so, it was probably John's elder brother James, who would have come back down Millbrook Lane and taken him to his own home in Leigh Lane.

Contrary to what Brickell had said, John was not buried in Knoyle. At the inquest, the coroner, Mr Whitmarsh, heard that the Yeomanry were stoned, had charged and when the rioters still resisted, opened fire. John Harding was said to have held on to the reins of one of the horses, while striking the rider with his stick. After five minutes the yeoman drew his pistol and shot him. The brother of the dead man (it seems likely to have been James) had come up to the witness and told him that John was dead.

The jury brought in a verdict of justifiable homicide. The coroner took this as being equivalent to suicide. Although he was sad to add to the suffering of the dead man's relatives, the law, he said, forbade him to issue a warrant for burial. In fact, John does appear in the Tisbury burial register.[13]

Justice, or at any rate the legal process, now moved swiftly. Depositions of witnesses were taken by local Justices of the Peace, including Henry Seymour at Knoyle House and John Benett himself at Pyt House. At the start of the trial in Salisbury, held by royal commission on New Year's Day 1831, Mr Justice Parkes addressed the Grand Jury. Their foreman was none other than John Benett Esq. MP and included William Wyndham Esq., MP and Commander of the Hindon Troop, as well as Wadham Wyndham who had accompanied him to Pyt House.

The judge, while recognising that rural poverty was a factor in the case, urged 'this highly respectable . . . body of the gentry of this county' to do their duty. The Grand Jury returned a 'True Bill' against 23 men, only 17 of whom were in custody, and the trial proper commenced. One man was acquitted by the 12 jurors and one was recommended for mercy. Of those convicted 14 were transported to Australia and did not return.

The available evidence makes it very likely that Knoyle men were among the rioters. However, they seem to have had the wit or good fortune not to be charged; for which their wives and families must have been grateful. Five privates from Knoyle were members of the Hindon Troop, 3 Squadron, Wiltshire Yeomanry Cavalry.[14] Thomas Flower, who later married Emma, lived in 'The Cottage', at the junction of Church Rails and Wise Lane. They had a daughter Mary. Thomas Stevens' and James King's addresses are not recorded, but Stevens married Hannah Scammell and they had three children: Ellen, George and Sidney. Charles Wigmore was probably from the same family group as James of Upper Leigh, who (as already described) was murdered in 1805. Private Jonathan Folliott, 36 years old, was part of the farming family of Knoyle Down and other local farms. His brother James evidently felt that some of those who took an active part might get off for lack of evidence. He therefore wrote to John Benett at Pyt House as follows:

> Sir, Not recollecting yesterday when I was at Pyt House, respecting the character of Norris he said the same evening when they returned home from Pyt House that he gave Benett a good one on the nose with a stone. He said this in the presence of severill people. I wrote this Sir fearing you might forgive him.
> I remain, Sir Your humble servt
> James Folliott

'Norris' could have been the husband of Ann Norris, who lived in a cottage opposite the *Seymour* (then the *Benett*) *Arms*.

The riots brought both condemnation and some sympathy for the agricultural poor. Wages were raised by a shilling (5p) a week. According to W.H. Hudson, author of *A Shepherd's Life* and collecting his material in the *Lamb Inn* at Hindon in 1909, when the fuss had died down they were reduced again – the farm workers once more learned a bitter lesson. Experienced married farmhands went back to seven shillings (35p) a week, while young unmarried men got four shillings (20p) or a little more, as did women.[15]

Sixty years later farm labourers working on Mr Percy Wyndham's farms in Knoyle got eleven shillings (55p) a week, with a head carter getting thireteen shillings and a shepherd fourteen. The members of the six-man threshing team working the machine got fourpence (under 2p) a day extra each, haymakers three shillings (15p) for a twelve-hour day and harvesters four shillings (20p) with some beer, for a thirteen-hour day.[16]

Georgian and Victorian Seymours at Knoyle House

O f the three prominent village families in Victorian times, the Seymours were the oldest established. Although the family had been based in Wiltshire since at least the 16th century, the first proven local connection comes with Sir Edward Seymour of Berry Pomeroy, whose portrait by Sir Peter Lely used to hang at Knoyle. He was elected MP for nearby Hindon in 1661, just after the Restoration of Charles II. He was elected Speaker of the House of Commons eleven years later.

The Speaker's fourth son was William, also an MP – for Totnes and elsewhere at various times. William's two wives are commemorated in the chancel of St. Mary's with a double wall tablet. This obliterated some of Dean Wren's plasterwork, so that of his 'Alpha' and 'Omega' panels, only the former remains. William's work is also ugly and disproportionately large.

The next head of the Knoyle family was Sir Francis Seymour, younger brother of Edward, 8th Duke of Somerset. He was MP for Great Bedwyn and later Marlborough. He married Elizabeth née Popham, Lady Hinchinbrooke – for some reason nicknamed 'Jenny Twitcher', and they had three children, Henry, Francis (who died young) and Mary.

By all accounts, Francis seems to have been an extraordinary individual. When Mary married John Bailey, a struggling farmer, she kept the wedding secret from her father. As soon as he found out, Francis turned her out saying that she had brought dishonour on the family name. However, he quickly began to regret his hasty action, for he missed the loving care and attention which she used to give him. He therefore reversed his decision. The couple were welcomed back home, offered £400 and given free board and lodging. When Mary produced a son, Francis became the proudest of grandfathers: 'The like of such a fine tall child has not been seen anywhere', he declared.

Sir Francis insisted on fixing each day's menu and his favourite dish was venison pasty. He was continually at odds with his son Henry; so much so that the young man stayed at a local inn when visiting Knoyle. Francis Seymour, formally described as 'of Trent and Sherborne' was buried at the ducal seat in Maiden Bradley.

Despite his difficulties with his father, son Henry did well for himself. He became a royal courtier with properties in Gloucestershire (Redland Court), Trent, Northbrook in Devon as well as Knoyle House. He was appointed Groom of the Bedchamber to George III, attending on him during his illness. He married Caroline Cowper, by whom he had two daughters. The elder, christened Caroline like her mother, married William Danby of Swinton Park in Yorkshire. The younger, Georgiana, became a diplomat's wife, marrying the last French Ambassador to the Venetian Republic before it was swallowed up by Napoleon.

Two years after Caroline died in 1773, Henry married again, this time to Louise, a widowed French countess. They had a son, Henry, who was a weakly boy. He was brought up by the housekeeper and only rarely saw his mother. During the Napoleonic wars he was 'detenu' in Paris, but given parole on condition that he promised not to leave the country. With the coming of peace he moved to Knoyle, where his health improved.

Henry Senior's involvement with the French aristocracy went beyond the Comtesse. He formed a dangerous alliance with the beautiful but illegitimate daughter of lower-class parents who had become Madame du Barry, mistress of the French King Louis XV. Du Barry wrote him the most extravagant love letters, but it all ended in tears. She was dismissed from the French court and banished to a nunnery when the King died in 1774. Nineteen years later, she was tried in a revolutionary court for 'wasting the treasures of the state' and wearing mourning for the late King Louis XVI, who had been executed a few months before. She was, predictably, found guilty, sentenced to death and died 'vainly whimpering' under the guillotine.

In 1802 Louise gave birth to a sister for Henry called Henriette, who grew up to display an ungovernable temper. She married James Tichborne, and produced a son called Roger. He was brought up in France, which he hated. Eventually, he escaped to England, giving the slip to a pursuer sent by his mother to drag him back.

Roger spent his holidays at Knoyle House as his uncle's guest. He liked a smoke, but Henry objected to people indulging this habit in his house. A special smoking parlour with its own entrance was therefore provided in another house on The Square, where he could entertain his friends.

Roger decided to join the Army. However, as his continental upbringing made him seem different from his fellows, he became the butt of cruel practical jokes. He resigned, with the intention of making a new life in Australia. He took ship in the *Bella*, but she foundered in a storm. Roger was never seen again.

Henriette was distraught, refusing to accept his death as a fact. She placed advertisements in Australian newspapers, prompting a succession of claimants to present themselves, hoping to inherit Tichborne Park after the death of Sir Alfred Tichborne, eleventh Baronet, in 1856. Eventually Arthur Orton, once a butcher in Wapping, but by then living in New South Wales at Wagga Wagga, came forward. Quick-witted and quite personable, he seems to have received such good coaching from a former family servant that he convinced Henriette that he was indeed her long lost son. This led to the famous case of 'The Tichborne Claimant'.

The once weakly Henry survived to marry Jane Hopkinson of Bath and to bring up five children before he died in 1849. His eldest son Henry Danby inherited other Seymour property, but Knoyle House went to his younger brother, Alfred.

Alfred Seymour of Knoyle, son of Henry Seymour of Knoyle and Trent(then in Somerset, now in Dorset). Lawyer, Member of Parliament, gambler and entrepreneur, he was not a man to suffer fools or knaves gladly. He was caring towards his family and treated his tenants fairly, earning their affection in return.

Somewhere about this time, the question of succession to the dukedom of Somerset became a matter of fierce debate in the family. The Duke, in an undated letter from his London residence at 28 Berkeley Square presumably to Henry and preserved in the Knoyle family papers, was very concerned. Jane Georgiana Sheridan, granddaughter of the famous Irish playwright, had married into the Seymour family. Mr Sheridan and his grandson-in-law ('The Sheridan Duke') along with Henry Thynne of the Longleat family, seem to have been targets of his fiercest wrath, and he was keen, in the biblical phrase, to visit their sins on the third and fourth generation.

The forthright letter reads:

By this will, if Lord Algernon's third son succeeds to the dukedom he will not inherit a single acre of Seymour property; he can starve no doubt, he can follow Mr Thynne's example, he can blow his brains out. For thirty years the Sheridan

Duke defrauded his sister, the executors did not dare defend him in open Court. He has stolen the family pictures, the plate, to leave them to the natural son of a tramp, who lived at one time, I am told, in a gipsy cart, on Bovey heath near Stover house in Devon. The hungry vermin, that low born beggar woman left behind her, defend this will, it is, they say, just, and honourable, they are worthy descendants of the drunken Irish blackguard, who wrote plays, told lies, cheated everybody, and died like a pig in a sty without a rag to cover him.

Alfred has been described as 'a lively and fashionable man and a great gambler'. He served as MP for Totnes, while his brother represented Poole. Alfred and Henry Danby shared a conviction in the value of a rail link between Salisbury and Yeovil. In 1854, the Salisbury & Yeovil Railway Company was incorporated, with the MP for Poole as its chairman. Two years later, there was a grand ceremony in a field at Gillingham: the *Illustrated London News* of 12th April 1856 described the scene:

> The first turf on the South West Central line was turned on 3 April 1856 under the most encouraging auspices. Notwithstanding the heavy rain, which began at an early hour and continued without the slightest intermission all day, the town of Gillingham saw a very great influx of visitors on the occasion . . . the ceremony of turning the first turf was performed by Miss Seymour, sister of the Honourable Member for Poole, the Chairman of the company.

Alfred Seymour's sister, Miss Sarah Ellen, turned the first turf of the South West Central railway line at Gillingham in heavy rain on the 3rd of April 1856. The ornate wheelbarrow which she trundled and the ceremonial silver spade are both to be seen in the Gillingham Museum. The spirit of the occasion was well captured by the Illustrated London News's *artist.*

'Miss Seymour' was probably Sara Ellen, the elder of the two unmarried Seymour daughters at the time.

The magazine accompanied its report with a graphic drawing showing the spectators huddled under umbrellas as the rain lashed down. The procession had just passed through a flag-bedecked triumphal arch and was led by a top-hatted gentleman bearing a ceremonial silver spade. Behind him Miss Seymour was bravely trundling an ornate walnut wheelbarrow; richly decorated with carved griffins' heads, sheaves of corn on the spokes and an array of coats of arms: The South Western Company, the Salisbury & Yeovil Railway Company, the Seymour family, Mr Locke and the contractor. She was somewhat shielded from the elements by another top-hatted gentleman holding an umbrella over her.

The first train steamed into Gillingham on the 2nd May 1859, but the remainder of the link to Yeovil took much longer. When some of the guarantors defaulted over the construction of this section, Alfred was forced to sell Clouds House in the village to his fellow MP, the Hon. Percy Wyndham, thereby creating a rival focus of society.

Soon, however, his finances recovered, though his offer to buy Clouds back was refused. The railway was duly completed and remains today; despite attempts in the Beeching era to reduce the whole line to single track, no doubt as a preliminary to closure.

Alfred had never believed that Arthur Orton was the rightful Tichborne heir, and from the moment that he became master of Knoyle, applied his energies to unmasking him – with great determination and attention to detail. For Orton's trial, he amassed a formidable array of evidence; producing photographs of Knoyle House on which the claimant could be minutely examined and even bringing the estate Game Book into court to refute claims that Orton had been present on particular shoots. One such photograph, reproduced here, was specially taken to show Roger's room and its immediate surroundings.

It took 103 days before Orton's claim collapsed and a further 188 days to convict him of perjury – the longest trial in English history at that time. Orton was sentenced to imprisonment for 14 years, being released in 1884. He finally confessed to the imposture three years before his death in 1898.

Alfred did not put up with incompetence if he could help it – a poor keeper got the sack because one day on a shoot 'the birds were very wild and unapproachable'. Retribution to unsatisfactory employees was echoed on one occasion by punishment for an ill-behaved dog. Brother-in-law Philip Pleydell-Bouverie, finding that a dog 'got in and spoiled the shooting', 'blazed at him and shot him in the posterior'! Poor shooting, even by members of his

On taking up his inheritance, Alfred Seymour set himself the task of exposing the man whom he(correctly)saw as an impostor laying claim to the Tichborne estate. This picture, of the room where the real Roger used to stay when a guest at Knoyle House, was specially taken for Orton's marathon trial.

close family, would be recorded for posterity in his estate Game Book. Thus, brother-in-law Sir Henry Rawlinson, although a General, was condemned because he, 'shot one dog, two keepers, Miss Guest and her horse, and perforated the game bags with numerous air holes'. One suspects that the language was rich on that occasion!

Alfred's interest in the bizarre led him to record in the Game Book an even more unsettling incident which took place on another estate at 'Ewerne' (Iwerne Minster), south of Shaftesbury on the Blandford road:

> At Ewerne near Shaston [a local name for Shaftesbury] a man killed at one shot a rabbit, a ferret and a child in a woman's arms, whose eye he also knocked out; the same discharge also shot out the eye of a man standing by.

Alfred was a great traveller. In 1852, for example, he left Knoyle for Russia just after Christmas and did not return until the end of the following summer, just in time for the shooting. In 1856, his tour took in Egypt, the Holy Land, Constantinople, the Crimea (where the Crimean War had just ended), Montenegro, Venice and Hungary – again returning in time for some autumn shooting.

On one notable occasion, shooting had to be put off until almost the end of September. This was because of the need for Alfred to support his brother Henry Danby's election campaign for the Poole parliamentary seat. The sacrifice was worth it, however, for Henry Danby 'was elected with glory on 24 September 1850'. Although of course constitutionally elected, Henry Danby could be quite authoritarian. In 1858 the village school had been erected on the edge of The Square opposite Knoyle House. When the 1870 Education Act was passed the room sizes were too small to be admissible, so a move or a rebuild became necessary. Henry Danby, along with the other residents of Knoyle House, found the noise made by the children so disturbing that, as Trustee of the great Seymour Estate, which at that time comprised half the village, he took decisive action. He gave a plot of land beyond the church and the Manor Farm (now the Village Hall), which he reckoned would be out of earshot.. In line with Rector Milford's strongly held views it was to be for, 'The education of the children of East Knoyle in the principles of the Established Church throughout England'.

Later on, when he suffered increasingly from chest ailments during the winter, he used to go abroad for Mediterranean holidays. The picture shown here is of Alfred with friends and members of his family in Algiers in the 1880s.

Alfred Seymour with members of his family in Algiers in about 1885. In his later years, he suffered badly from chest ailments. Like many after him, he sought to exchange the English winter for Mediterranean sun.

The image of a harsh, intolerant man is softened by his caring attitude towards those who served him well, and by the genuine affection he seems to have inspired in his tenants. An early example of this was demonstrated when Alfred brought his bride home to Knoyle in 1866. The *Western Gazette* had the story:

> the village and neighbourhood were . . . scenes of great excitement. There was a plentiful display of flags at Semley station and a troop of horsemen, splendidly mounted, tenants on the Knoyle estate, and friends, were drawn up beside a triumphant arch to welcome the happy pair. The mounted gentlemen accompanied the carriages from the station to Knoyle three miles distant and all along there were signs of the goodwill of the inhabitants, who had displayed great taste in the erections of the arches and decking their windows with flowers. Bouquets were thrown to the bride as she passed. On arrival at Knoyle nearly the whole population, about 1,200, were assembled, the bells pealed merrily and the farmers and labourers afterwards sat down to dinner.

When he died of apoplexy in 1888, after battling against a succession of illnesses, the tenants placed a fine memorial window in the north aisle of the church. Probably executed by Powell & Co., with Holliday as the artist, it depicts Simeon in the Temple at Jerusalem, with Mary and the infant Jesus.

The tablet below simply reads:

> To the Sacred Memory of
> Alfred Seymour of Knoyle House
> This window is erected
> By his Tenantry who loved him.

His obituary in the Parish Magazine testifies to a warm humanity:

> We have lost the kindliest of friends in Mr Seymour, whom after many months of feeble health and suffering, which he bore with unfailing cheerfulness and remarkable patience, God called to his rest on March 15th. He was the friend of all; for all he had a pleasant word and cheerful greeting; to all he was ready to lend a helping hand; the outcome of his warm and unselfish heart . . .

After his death, Knoyle House passed eventually to Alfred and Isabella's only child Jane Margaret, born in 1873. The property was, however, let to a succession of tenants. The first was Lord Stalbridge, a member of the Grosvenor family, and the last tenant to live in it as a private residence was Beatrix, Dowager Countess of Pembroke, who arrived in 1914 and was for thirty years the last 'Squire' of the village.

Sadly, Jane became mentally ill, so that the estate had to be placed in the hands of trustees. The last of the Seymours of Knoyle died in 1943.

Miss Jane Seymour, the last of the Seymours of Knoyle. Born in 1873, she was only 15 when her father died. She developed a mental illness, so that administration of the estate passed to trustees. She died in 1943.

The Wyndhams

Since at least 1740, the Seymours had been the leading family in Knoyle, but even before Alfred's death in 1888, this position had been at least partially usurped by the Wyndhams.

Percy Scawen Wyndham was the younger surviving son of George, first Lord Leconfield and his wife Mary. They were a strange pair, but in life and in his will, George favoured Percy over his elder brother Henry. Thus, though Henry inherited Petworth Park and the title on his father's death, Percy received a very generous inheritance to add to the gifts already bestowed upon him by his doting father. This was, not surprisingly, a source of lasting resentment.

As soon as his education at Eton was completed, Percy gained a commission in the Coldstream Guards, rising to the rank of Captain. His London posting was a not too arduous round of barrack and ceremonial duties, interspersed with an active social life in the capital and in country houses.

The onset of the Crimean War brought the partying to an abrupt end. In the spring of 1854, his battalion took ship for Scutari, with a welcome stop off at Malta. A pleasant six-week interlude passed before orders were given to occupy Varna in Bulgaria. Camp was pitched on a slimy, marshy waste outside the town. The filthy, insanitary conditions soon took their toll as men began to fall sick in droves. Two further moves took the unit to Guereklek, where cholera was added to the other ills. Percy himself collapsed and was invalided home before the remnant of the unit set off to campaign at the front in the Crimea.

Percy's brief military career ended with his retirement in November. Five years later, he met the beautiful Madeline Campbell while visiting his brother-in-law at the Chief Secretary's lodge in Phoenix Park, Dublin. She was the daughter of the late Major General Sir Guy Campbell; who had died in 1849, leaving his widow with a pension of just £600 a year. Sir Guy had held two senior army posts in Ireland. His father-in-law, Lord Edward Fitzgerald, had also had a military career, serving with distinction in the American War of

Independence. Since that time, he had married Madeline's mother Pamela who was, perhaps, a daughter of Madame de Genlis by Philippe 'Egalité', Duke of Orleans. Of more vital concern, he had taken up the Irish revolutionary cause, tried to arrange for a French invasion of Ireland in 1796, and been betrayed and seized in Dublin. In the scuffle he received wounds from which he later died.

As Caroline Dakers succinctly put it: Madeline Campbell 'had no money, no property and no detractors'. Despite the misdemeanours of Percy's cousin Wilfrid Scawen Blunt, their love match endured. The marriage in 1860, in many ways a fusion of opposites, ripened into over half a century of happily married life.

With a London house and Cockermouth Castle, in what became his parliamentary constituency and which he served as member for 25 years until 1885, life was comfortable for Percy, Madeline and their growing family. On his father's death in 1869, Percy was no longer welcomed at Petworth, and Cockermouth Castle passed to his brother. A replacement in the Lake District was found at Isel, thanks to the good offices a local landowner. However, when his financial circumstances made it possible, a search was made for a suitable country house down south.

The opportunity arose when Alfred Seymour's finances came under pressure in the mid-1870s, partly through the failure of some of the guarantors in his railway company. He was forced to sell off most of the northern half of his estate, including the windmill, much of Milton, several farms and 'Clowdes', a rather charming Georgian house named after John Cloud (or Clowde), who lived in an earlier property on the site in 1581. Clowdes had only become Seymour property in 1828, when Henry bought it from the executors of James Charles Still. The Stills were descendants of a famous Bishop of Bath and Wells. Their family tomb stands just to the north of the St. Mary's chancel. There is a fine eagle lectern in memory of 200 years of Still family residence. What is now the Cross chapel restored in memory of the 20th-century rector Canon Cross was formerly named after the Stills, the last of whom – one Captain Still – lived at Slades and was a sitting tenant in 1876.

The sale of the Clowdes site was particularly galling to Alfred Seymour, as he had selected it as the most suitable position for the new country house which he was planning and which was eventually erected on the east side of The Square, in the centre of the village. He got as far as having Edward Blore draw up plans for a mansion in the Gothic revival style, before he had to abandon the project.

Alfred's misfortune was Percy's opportunity. He could see the potential of the site: it gave a fine prospect to the south and yet the main frontages were, and are, secluded from the public view – especially since the 'New Road' was built along the upper slopes of the valley lying to the north up past the windmill.

The purchase was barely completed when Alfred's business affairs took a turn for the better. He tried to buy back 'Clouds' as the Wyndhams were always to call it from then on, but Percy was by now too deeply immersed in turning his dreams into reality to consider the idea.

The architect chosen was Philip Webb, a partner in William Morris's firm of Morris & Co., which was later to make Clouds a showpiece for the ideas of the Arts & Crafts Movement. Percy's financial resources were not limitless. Although a London firm was initially favoured to build the house, in the end the contract went to Albert Estcourt of Gloucester, whose costs were about 20% lower. Webb's reluctance to employ anyone other than a London contractor was not due to pigheadedness, but because he was a perfectionist and worried that the standards he sought could only be found in the metropolis. The go-ahead finally came in 1881, when the Georgian house had been demolished and work commenced. It was completed four years later at a cost of £80,000 – a vast sum in those days. The architect combined traditional, classical and Gothic Revival styles to make an impressive whole. Even in its present cut down form, the building combines an impression of size and status without great ostentation. It is still possible to imagine it as a dignified yet genuine family home.

The materials used for the exterior were local green sandstone, such as that quarried on Cleeve in the north of the village area and to be seen on many surviving buildings; together with tiles, brown weatherboarding and red brick. Inside, the decor was striking. Instead of following the heavily curtained fashion of the period, the outstanding skillls of artists such as Burne-Jones, the motifs of the Arts and Crafts movement being created by Morris & Co. and the taste of Madeline Wyndham in particular combined to produce something special. There were plasterwork friezes, white picture-hung walls relieved by an occasional William Morris pattern, unstained oak, a wall painting of angels by the staircase from the hand of Burne-Jones himself, good 18th-century furniture and William Morris upholstery. This fitted in with a vast amount of oriental porcelain in blue and white, vases of flowers and all manner of antiques and curios. The whole decorative scheme was generally admired as being in perfect taste.

Towards the end of the construction period, a mysterious event occurred, long remembered in the village and quoted by Wilfrid Blunt in an article he wrote for *Country Life*. A lady in black had been noticed coming down the road from the windmill, watching the work going on. Neil, a workman who later worked for Webb's assistant Detmar Blow, is said to have been approached by her at the west door and asked a number of questions: about the owner, the architect, the builder and so on. Finally she asked to look at the work inside – which she was permitted to do. Having looked round the hall she said, 'This house will be burnt down, and in less than three years'. She went outside again, and vanished. In Edith Olivier's account, the 'mysterious old woman' was clothed in shabby black and delivered her warning 'holding up her hand like some ancient sorceress'. The Wyndhams were unaware of the incident. Nobody took much notice at the time and the lady was wrong about when the disaster would happen. However, otherwise her utterance proved to be prophetic.

The Fire

In the South of England, we have become used over the past few years to a succession of mild winters. The Christmas and New Year season of 1888-89 was however traditional Victorian Christmas card weather, the coldest for a generation.

There have been several accounts written of the fire which broke out early on Sunday morning 6th January. That by Edith Olivier in her chapter on Madeline Wyndham in her book *Four Victorian Ladies of Wiltshire* paints a very graphic picture which ties in with the others examined in all essential detail. It is reproduced below with the permission of both the publisher and Edith's niece, the late Miss Rosemary Olivier.

> A sleepy servant put into a housemaid's cupboard a scuttleful of ashes which she had just scraped out of a fireplace the night before. Unfortunately they were not all dead, and there was paper in the scuttle too. By seven o'clock the whole house was ablaze, the fire roaring up through the great central hall, which went sheer from the ground floor to the roof. It made a perfect funnel through which a strong current of air drove the flames with incredible force. When it was discovered, little could be done. There were then no telephones. The telegraph service did not operate at night. Salisbury was twenty miles away, and Mere, the nearest place, was separated from Clouds by roads which were practically impassable through the frost.

Although Olivier does not record it, the Mere Brigade did manage to get through before any other appliances could arrive. There was, however, a delay before they could operate their pump. This was because the pond at

Waterdale, just North of Clouds in the Milton valley, was frozen solid. To continue:

Grooms on galloping horses went out from the stables and scoured the country for the fire engines which . . . were only adapted for very small village fires. So while the fire roared on uninterrupted, it took hours to reach the nearest horse-drawn engines, one of which was stationed at Salisbury and another at Wilton, where Lord Pembroke had an estate fire brigade. The Pembrokes were close friends of the Wyndhams. No-one could be more willing to send help, but the difficulties were beyond anything we can imagine today [the author was writing in 1945]. Clouds stands above Wilton by more than the height of Salisbury spire, and the hills between the two places are very steep. The roads that morning were like glass, and three times in the course of that eighteen-mile journey the horses fell on a specially steep gradient, and were too badly hurt to go on. They were replaced by fresh teams, borrowed from nearby farms. Thus reinforced they sped along again, slipping and sliding about the roads, and seeing ahead of them, all the time, the enormous pillar of fire which Clouds had now become. When they arrived it was almost a hopeless case, for the fire had got full possession and the flames appeared almost to reach the sky. It was still freezing so hard that the Captain of the Wilton brigade – a gigantic man of great strength – was almost frozen to death as he stood on the roof directing the hose. To anyone watching from the ground, his figure was clearly silhouetted against the fire in the background. After a time it appeared to lose its mobility and erect carriage. What had happened to Captain Carse? A fireman approached him, and took his arm. It was completely stiff. And it then transpired that his clothes, which were saturated with water, had turned to ice even in the midst of the fire and Carse was frozen on to the side of the ladder up which he had climbed.

Meanwhile the household, the estate men, and the village people all played their parts. The family escaped by the skin of their teeth. Some small grandchildren were in the nursery at the very top of the house, and they were swathed in wet blankets with sponges in their mouths, and carried downstairs by their nurses, whose shoes were all but burnt through on the red-hot stairs.

The village people rushed in and out of the burning building, dragging out everything that they thought of value. The priceless furniture and *objets d'art* were heaped helter-skelter in the garden . . . the billiard table was tenderly salvaged and lugged out on to the lawn. At all the bedroom windows there appeared the determined faces of distracted housemaids hurling the jugs and basins and bedroom crockery down from the top floors to the ground, till Mrs Wyndham interrupted this well-meant though disastrous clatter, by saying that she thought it was not worth while to 'save any more china'.

As the pale winter sun came up over the garden, she was seen standing a little way off from the ruins of the house, with a rapt look on her face, as she watched the glorious curved tongues of flame which leapt from the burning walls into the sky. She had thrown a rough homespun coat over her nightgown, and the lace frills escaped beneath the tweed sleeves and fell over her hands which were flung out in an unconscious gesture of wonder at the sight. She was entranced by its beauty and terror.

Although no lives were lost, 'Nothing was left but a grand ruin', as the Rector noted in his parish magazine, 'which no one could forget, though he live to be an old man'.

It was now that Percy and Madeline showed their mettle. With the insurance companies meeting their obligations and paying up, funds were available; though the magnitude of the task would have daunted most people. Not so the Wyndhams. The architect Philip Webb and the former workers were re-engaged and set to work using the original plans. Just 32 months later the house was reoccupied. During this time, the family occupied the servants' accommodation. Although there was little modern plumbing, it was otherwise pretty comfortable. This was thanks to Philip Webb's socialist concepts, for he had built in standards of space and comfort far in advance of the accepted standards of the day.

The Clouds Estate Fire Brigade attending a fire at Broad Oaks, Semley in about 1920. On the ground: William Mallett Captain, J Gray Engineer, E Ford Fireman; On near side of engine: C Allen 2nd Officer, W Snook Fireman, J Beale Fireman, B Gray Fireman; On off side of engine: E Mallett 3rd Officer, W Mallett Fireman, S Coles Fireman, Coachman J Pearson.

Not wishing to be caught a second time, Percy set up his own fire brigade – with his Clerk of Works William Mallett as Captain. He and his family lived at Park Cottage, Milton Green to which a fire alarm bell was fixed. Bertha Mallett, his daughter, used to tell of keen competition among the children to ring the bell, for which a fee of one shilling was paid (5p – a worthwhile sum in those days). There was a second bell hung at Bell Cottage on The Square. As an alternative, a telegram would be sent to Clouds (!). The horses could be harnessed within ten minutes and the crew, drawn from the estate workers, became very proficient.

Shortly after World War I the horse-drawn manual type fire engine was acquired by the village and housed at Knoyle House stables. It was manned by a newly reformed fire brigade.

In the event of a fire alarm being raised, the arrangement was to call on Bill Turner (who lived at Church Rails) to bring along his horse to haul the engine. Mr George King, who lived as a boy in a cottage (now demolished) in Wise Lane and whose grandfather George Smith had been a mason working for the Seymours, recalled one occasion in the early 1920s when the brigade was summoned to attend a fire at a house in the next door village, Sedgehill. It was late at night when Bill Turner went to Park Mead, the field opposite the church, to catch his horse by the light of a candle lantern. The horse thought this a most irregular proceeding and would have none of it. Meanwhile the firemen had become anxious; so, realising the urgency to get to the fire, they pushed the engine to Sedgehill by hand. It seems that they were in time to save a part of the house, and Bill Turner arrived in time to haul the engine back to Knoyle.

In its latter days the brigade's Captain was Mr J Elliot who lived in Bell Cottage on The Square. The unit continued to function until 1940, when it was absorbed into the national Auxiliary Fire Service. When the appliance was replaced by a motor engine, the old machine was presented to the Parish Council. For a while it was kept near the old Clouds water tower. Its present whereabouts (if it still exists) are unknown, though there has been a suggestion that it went to Wilton . . .

Percy and Madeline

The most obvious side of the Honourable Percy Scawen Wyndham's character was his fiery temper. His colourful language was peppered with the obscenities and blasphemies which were commonplace in his youth; but which had gone out of fashion in polite society by the later years of Queen Victoria's reign.

For those in a position to answer him back, his outbursts were – in his granddaughter Cynthia Asquith's words – 'nearly always followed by his leading the burst of laughter against himself . . . frowns and smiles constantly overlapped one another.'

The East Knoyle Band, though generally popular and in demand for dances and public events, also caught the rough edge of his tongue on one occasion. It was the band's custom to start out at midnight on Christmas Eve to visit all the big houses, farms and inns, returning perhaps a trifle unsteadily to The Square at about 6 a.m. At Clouds one day, Mr Wyndham called the Bandmaster over and asked him what he meant by waking up people in the middle of the night. 'I, personally, did not hear you, but my guests did and said you made a horrible noise'.

Even the animal kingdom was not immune from criticism. On one long remembered occasion, he pinned up a notice which read 'The cuckoo *must not sing* in the Western woods'!

He was also extremely obstinate. On one occasion, he was heard to mutter to himself, with just a touch of wry amusement 'I *must* do what I like, I *must* do what I like'.

Although always smartly turned out, his dress sense remained rooted in the early years of Victoria's reign. On Sundays, in spongebag trousers and top hat, he led his family into church and took his place in the front pew, specially fitted with blue cushions while the rest of the pews were bare.

Mrs Hubert (Florence) Tanswell, who lived at The Green and died in 1984, aged 88, remembered sitting behind the Wyndhams in church and being fascinated by the bald patch on Percy's head. Fascination was mixed with apprehension; for the subject of her interest was liable to turn round, fix an eyeglass in his eye, and view the congregation with a basilisk stare. Happily, Florence was never caught. She remained a regular churchgoer for the rest of her life. Despite increasing disability in her later years, she was always properly robed as a chorister. Her treble singing voice remained clear and true well into her eighties.

Dedicated to his family, Percy reserved any display of tenderness or affection for the privacy of his home. He inspired a fierce loyalty in those who worked for him; even though he had been known to blast off at his gamekeeper in moments of frustration after missing his target.

As demonstrated in the rebuilding of his house after the fire Percy Wyndham had marked ability in getting things done over. Disturbed by the way in which so many churches were being ruthlessly 'restored' by over-enthusiastic Victorian architects he translated his feelings into support for the Society for the Protection of Ancient Buildings (SPAB) when this was founded by William Morris in 1877. Percy became a Committee Member.

In 1891, the church tower was in a very poor state, with demolition being considered as the only course open. Percy approached Philip Webb, SPAB's first President for help. In consequence, the Society accepted the task of restoration as one of its first major projects.

Webb gave his services free. Under his direction, with help from Detmar Blow and with Frank Green from the village as foreman mason, the delicate task was undertaken. Much of the tower's rubble and stone filling was carefully removed from the inside and replaced, with a certain amount of new brickwork added. Where necessary, a tile on end was slipped almost imperceptibly into the outer stonework. From the outside the tower looked almost untouched, so that some of the contributors to the cost even wondered how their money had been spent. The original estimate turned out to be too low. The Wyndhams made a generous initial donation, adding to it in order to help meet the overrun which brought the total to £1400.

In public affairs, though he held strong opinions, Percy Wyndham was regarded as a fair man who set high standards. This was shown in the way that he directed the management of his estate, as well as in his work as a magistrate. These qualities earned him the respect of his architect. Webb was a very talented man with strong views himself. However, he found the Wyndhams ready to consider new ideas and positive in their approach.

D.E. Little, writing for the Women's Institute Village Scrapbook, commented that 'Everyone stood in awe of Mr Percy Wyndham, but not of dear Mrs Wyndham, who was kind to all'. Certainly, every reference consulted agreed that she was loved and respected by everyone with whom she came in contact – family, friends and the people of the village. Edith Olivier summed it up by writing of Percy's bride:

> Madeline Campbell was a captivating jumble of genius, beauty, and charm, derived from her mixed French, Irish, Scottish, and English ancestry. As life went on, her vital spirit compounded this legacy of varied qualities into a personality rich in intelligence, sympathy and wit. She had in fact every characteristic which could make a perfect hostess . . . A fete in the village was as enjoyable for her as a society function in London . . . She knew how to draw people out and make them at their best; although she never kept the centre of the stage for herself.

Madeline was an accomplished artist in her own right, in three separate disciplines. She was a competent painter in landscapes as well as depicting interiors at Petworth House. She designed and executed embroidery; being instrumental with her husband in founding the School of Art Needlework, which came under royal patronage in 1875. Finally, as a pupil of Alexander Fisher, she acquired the technique of enamelling on metal.

All the village schoolchildren were invited up to Clouds twice a year. The Christmas Party always featured a Punch & Judy show, with a conjuror often in attendance as well. Prizes were given for good school attendance.

The Summer Feast was also an eagerly anticipated occasion. There are two surviving accounts of the 1888 feast held on 25th August: one by the Rector and one by Madeline herself in a letter to her newly married daughter Madeline (Mrs Adeane). The children who attended either the Day or the Sunday School assembled at the school at 1.30 and marched up to Clouds. After being greeted with a bun and a pear on arrival, all sorts of toys were provided for the younger children to play with: trumpets and other musical instruments, reins, whips, skipping ropes, flags and footballs. The older boys played cricket, while a 'splendid band' (it is not recorded whether this was the East Knoyle one) played on the terrace.

Tea for the adults was served indoors, who were entertained by Miss Pamela Wyndham with her mandolin while they were waiting. The children attacked the piles of food laid out on long tables in the garden. Afterwards, there were three-legged, sack and ordinary races, followed by scrambling for nuts and apples. Each child then filed past Mrs Wyndham and received a bag of sweets and a bun to sustain them on the return journey. She praised the children for their good behaviour and said she was glad they had enjoyed themselves. Hearty cheers were given for Mr and Mrs Wyndham, the Rector and Mrs Milford, Mr Tanswell (the Headmaster), Miss Minns (his Assistant) 'and everyone imaginable'. The guests then dispersed.

One fancy which Percy indulged was his liking for a game of golf – so he built a nine hole course towards the A303. This was known as the 'political' course, for each hole was given the name of a politician. Many of the 'Souls' used to enjoy a round, in the course of which they would pause for lunch at a shelter constructed of furze.

Even as a widow, Madeline continued to take her social duties seriously. When Bertha, William Mallett's daughter, was about to be married to Gerald Forward in 1916, five years after Percy died, she sent her a letter of good wishes. Written in pencil on black-edged mourning paper it recalled the 'wonderful goodness' of William and his wife as an example to be closely followed. It was signed 'Your true friend for your Father's and Mother's sake – Madeline Wyndham.' Gerald Forward farmed Upton Farm with his brother Ivan. Sadly George and Bertha did not have long together, for he was one of those who did not return from the First World War, dying on the eve of the Armistice. His widow survived him by 63 years. On her death, this letter became the treasured possession of Bertha's daughter, Mrs Mary Hall, who was born at Park Cottage herself.

As a husband and wife team, Percy and Madeline complemented each other to make Clouds a magnet for that select group of intelligent aristocrats banding together in the mid-1880s, who came to be known as 'The Souls', though they themselves disliked the name.

Perhaps the grandest was Lord Curzon, Viceroy of India for seven years from 1898. At the centre of the circle was fellow Old Etonian Arthur J Balfour, later to become Prime Minister. Women were equally as welcome as men, provided that they had beauty, intelligence and wit. Within the group there was no 'generation gap' of mistrust and non-comprehension.

This was certainly true of the Wyndhams. Percy and Madeline added lustre to the group, as did their son George and daughter Mary. Mary's personality was too much for one 'non-Soul' admirer. In Jane Abdy and Charlotte Gere's lively study of the group 'The Souls', this young man is recorded as remarking of the young debutante 'She's a very nice filly, but she's read too many books for me'.

The accepted mid-Victorian code of moral rectitude, and in particular the seventh commandment: 'Thou shalt not commit adultery', was not always observed in 'Souls' society. Affaires with married women were not necessarily condemned; although it was considered important that the early children of a marriage should be true born to protect the blood line. Husbands would usually agree to give their name to children born from an irregular liaison.

Literature, music and art were all appreciated by the group, members of whom commissioned pictures by such as Burne-Jones, Watts and Whistler. It was to the American John Singer Sargent that Percy turned for a portrait of his three daughters: Mary (Lady Elcho), Pamela (Mrs Tennant) and Madeline (Mrs Adeane). Unusually, Sargent painted his sitters at their London home instead of in his studio. In the background he included Watts's 1877 portrait of their mother, which most people felt did not do her justice.

Exhibited at the Royal Academy in 1900, it immediately became a focus of attention. This focus was sharpened when the Prince of Wales (afterwards Edward VII), speaking at the Academy dinner, nicknamed the painting 'The Three Graces' – by which name it has been known ever since. Percy's grandson Dick sold the picture in 1927. It now hangs in the Metropolitan Museum of Art, New York.

The Family

All five of Percy and Madeline's children were born in London. In contrast to most Victorian families of the time, their upbringing was remarkably free and easy. This was designed to increase their creativity, which it did; but it also tended to induce a lack of self-discipline. Both parents were devoted to their children and the love was fully returned. They were fortunate to have the services as governess of Fräulein Schneider (known as 'Bun') who was very much part of the family. She was one of those who rushed to save the children on the top floor when Clouds caught fire. She carried Mary Elcho's daughter Cynthia to safety, and was invited to be her godmother. She remained with the family until the outbreak of World War I. She was a great lover of England, but saw nothing inconsistent in inviting the Wyndham children to contribute their pennies to a collecting box to build a battleship for the Kaiser, a project being supported by the women of Germany!

For all its size, Clouds was a happy family home. Grand-daughter Cynthia (Asquith) remembers it as 'alive with dogs, cushioned baskets contained grinning fox-terriers in every room – and the whole place was an aviary. Peacocks and laughing jackasses strutted and shrieked, doves, rooks and all manner of garden birds flocked to the house for the food that Madeline put out each morning.

In a display of his versatility, Percy and Madeline's son George wrote a poem to celebrate the rebuilding of Clouds after the fire, which was beautifully illustrated by his mother. The story line was that of a rook, who, having benefited from Madeline's generosity in providing food for him and the other birds during a very hard winter, had decided to stay around as a mark of respect. Madeline dedicated the poem to her grandchildren, and a number of copies of 'The Ballad of Mr Rook' are in the village archive.

'The Ballad of Mr. Rook' written by George and illustrated by his mother for the Wyndham grandchildren. It is the delightful tale of a rook, grateful for Mrs Wyndham's kindness over a hard winter. The Windmill and Clouds can be made out in the background.

One dog, belonging to Henry (Lord Leconfield) played a significant part in Wyndham family relations. After years of antipathy, Henry was persuaded to put aside his resentment at the favour shown to his younger brother. A visit to Clouds for the weekend was accordingly arranged. With commendable restraint being shown on both sides, the reconciliation between Henry and Percy was going well. All this was suddenly thrown into disarray when Henry's dog took it into his head to bite the master of the house!

Percy's favourite was undoubtedly his elder son and heir. George was handsome, artistic, romantic, articulate, well educated and intelligent. His love of literature competed with his enthusiasm for Territorial soldiering as a member of

George Wyndham, Percy's son and heir. Multi-talented with a rare understanding of Irish affairs, his time as the master of Clouds was to last only a little over two years.

the Cheshire Yeomanry; but more sharply with the demands of a political career that promised much and almost achieved it.

Percy came close to idolising his brilliant son. Family and guests at the dinner table, no matter how eminent, could be silenced by Percy holding up his hand to demand silence and saying 'Shush, shush, George is going to speak'.

George's life was lived at breakneck speed, both figuratively and almost literally. He was a reckless rider with a passion for hunting, though not simply to outwit the fox or from any blood lust. His niece, Cynthia, quotes him as saying after a long day in the saddle around Knoyle: 'I hunted for six immortal hours of galloping and singing to my horse when he was tired, and I was jubilant. . . The music of the hounds . . . made my blood sing.'

George married the beautiful young widow Sibell, Lady Grosvenor in 1887, becoming MP for Dover two years later. While a good stepfather to her children, he was devoted to his own son Percy Lyulph, always known as 'Perf'.

Very effective in private discussion, his speeches in the House of Commons sometimes suffered from trying to cram too many ideas into too small a compass.

The pinnacle of his political career came with his appointment as Chief Secretary for Ireland, where he had worked before as Private Secretary to Balfour. With his Irish background, foresight and political courage, he made notable headway at first. His great achievement was to secure the passage of a Land Bill which, as his successor Walter Long put it: 'will ever stand as an enduring monument to his statesmanship and great insight into Irish difficulties and Irish character.'

The royal visit to Dublin by King Edward VII and Queen Alexandra in 1903 was an undoubted success, but thereafter misfortune, miscalculations and stress-related illness led Balfour to dismiss him. Despite this, he retained his parliamentary seat of Dover in the 1906 election, when Conservative fortunes sank very low.

There were happy times at Knoyle at the end of 1908 when Perf celebrated his coming of age. The actual birthday was on 5th December, but the public celebrations took place after Christmas. On 29th December Percy hosted a 'lawn meet' of the South & West Wilts Hunt, dispensing generous hospitality before a leisurely start.

The much photographed 'lawn meet' of the South & West Wilts Hunt at Clouds on December the 29th 1908, held as part of the 21st birthday celebrations for 'Perf' Wyndham.

On Tuesday and Wednesday 12th-13th January there were two days of festivities. On the Tuesday evening at 6 p.m. the household servants assembled in the central hall. Mr Icke, the butler, and Miss Simnett, the housekeeper, presented Perf with a handsome inscribed clock. They were prompted to do so, said Mr Icke, 'by the great respect in which you, your parents and your grandparents are held by myself and my fellow servants.' Perf thanked them and 'proceeded to shake hands and exchange a kindly word with each of the contributors'. An hour later it was the tenants' turn. After appropriate toasts, Mr Jacob, the oldest tenant, handed over a pair of George I silver candlesticks. He was very pleased that Perf had some good old English sporting blood in his veins – they would always try to find a good straight-necked fox for him. In his reply Perf thanked them and said that the Army was his profession (he now held a commission in the Coldstream Guards) and foxhunting was his pleasure – and he hoped that foxhunting would go on as long as the country. The evening finished with an entertainment.

Next day, the employees and their wives were entertained to dinner in a marquee on the lawn. Their gift was a beautiful massive silver cup, based on an old Irish design. This time Perf remarked to laughter that he was in a profession which did not require brainy men perhaps – but one the country could not do without. He would be very pleased if some of the young men present would join up, because he believed it would do them good. At dusk, a firework display and a servants' ball in the marquee brought proceedings to an end.

Percy and Madeline celebrated their golden wedding anniversary on the 16th October 1910. There was a family house party, the present of a silver rose bowl from the tenants and a much appreciated gold-mounted fountain pen from the schoolchildren subscribed for with their pennies and halfpennies.

The Wyndhams now gave thought to a suitable burial plot in the new cemetery above the rectory, where the south-east corner was set aside for the purpose. Madeline set about designing the central cross. Soon afterwards Percy died peacefully in his sleep on 13th March 1911. His body was cremated and the ashes sent back to Knoyle for burial. They were contained in an oak coffer made from wood grown on the estate. This rested in the chancel of the church overnight before the service, with many village people taking the opportunity to pay their last respects. Drawn blinds, a massive attendance of family, Clouds staff, village people and visitors, a moving service, muffled bells, and a sense of loss – all marking the passing of an era.

George now assumed control. In the next two years he was very busy in Knoyle. He created a long library running the whole width of the house from a suite of bedrooms. Detmar Blow produced designs for the panelling bookcases and architectural fittings, but George modified these to his own taste and that of his mother. The actual work was entrusted to William Mallett;

Percy and Madeline Wyndham photographed in front of Clouds on their Golden Wedding day, October the 16th 1910. Percy was to die within six months, but Madeline survived for another decade.

who used oak grown on the estate. He also converted the former lamp room in the basement into a barrel-vaulted chapel for Madeline.

George then set himself to complete the family memorial burial plot. William Mallett is said to have overruled Detmar Blow's ideas 'as usual'. He was clearly very much in charge of the building and maintenance department at this period. Madeline's tutor, Alexander Fisher, was to design a grave surround for George himself, as well as a very fine and beautiful plate for Guy Wyndham's wife Minnie. Fisher's work is now in poor condition. Although the lawn contractor in the New Cemetery and some local residents try to keep some semblance of order in the memorial plot, it is in a sad state.

Mr Gordon Chambers, a churchwarden who was tireless in his work for church and village, approached the family some years ago for financial support to maintain the plot; but the response was disappointing. The wall at the southern end of the memorial had spaces to accommodate memorials to future generations, but the deaths in action of five of Madeline's grandsons during World War I are responsible for the fact that no future generations are recorded there. Alexander Fisher designed the wall plate to these men beside the pulpit in the church.

George lived to see his only son 'Perf' married to Diana Lister, but his own death followed soon afterwards, shortly before his 50th birthday. Although his wife Sibell forgave him his affaire with Gay, Lady Plymouth, which continued until his death, the actual circumstances of his passing in Paris in June 1913 remain obscure, with more than one version circulating in the family. The account published by his brother Guy speaks of a visit to his stepson the Duke of Westminster, known (from the heraldic description of his coat of arms) as 'Bend Or'. In company with the writer Hilaire Belloc, he had been out to St. Germain and the Buzneval woods. The next morning, 8th June, he woke with chest pains and was advised by the doctor to stay quiet for a few days and delay his return home to Clouds. The pain continued, so a nurse gave him an injection of morphia, which settled him ready for sleep. By the evening he was dead, due to a clot of blood reaching the heart. He was buried at Knoyle on the 13th June, in the new family plot. He was a remarkable man, who would still have had much to offer both his country and the community at Clouds.

His parliamentary colleagues in both Houses marked their appreciation of his life and work by commissioning a fine east window for the church from Sir Ninian Comper. With fine colour renderings, the subjects depicted reflect his family, his English and Irish connections. The artist 'signed' his work with his 'trade mark', a strawberry plant, together with the date (1915) by the hem of the Virgin Mary's robe. The window was not installed and dedicated until 1934.

Perf's marriage to the Honourable Diana Lister was celebrated on 17th April 1913. Within 18 months he would be dead. World War I began on 4th August 1914. As a professional officer with the Coldstream Guards, he was sent to France as part of the British Expeditionary Force (BEF), comprising seven divisions: six infantry and one cavalry. Within a month the Allies fought the Battle of the Marne, forcing a German retreat which eased the imminent threat to Paris. At Soissons Perf's battalion was ordered to attack across the River Aisne towards Lâon as part of an offensive by the BEF, supported by the French 5th Army on their right. The Germans had a strong position, their morale was good and they were very well armed. The fighting was savage, with the opposing forces pouring concentrated artillery and small arms into each other at close

George and Sibell's son: Lt Percy Lyulph Wyndham, always known as 'Perf'. Amiable and well liked by the Clouds staff, he was a keen professional soldier, commissioned into the Coldstream Guards. Sent over to France as part of the British Expeditionary Force at the outbreak of World War I, he was killed within weeks. He died bravely, leading his men in an attack across the River Aisne against a strongly held German position.

range, in the latter case, sometimes as little as ten or twenty yards. The carnage was appalling. Although there were many enemy dead around them, Perf and his men had little chance of survival. 'Bend Or', who was also at Soissons, wrote to George Wyndham's widow: 'He is at rest . . . He lies in a little wood where he has done so well.'

The youngest of Percy and Madeline's children was christened Pamela Adelaide Genevieve. Probably the most beautiful of 'The Three Graces', she was certainly the most favoured by her parents. She was articulate and well-read. She had a talent for literary expression, her entertaining letters being passed round the family to read. She could be excellent company, except when in one of what her friend Violet Milford called 'her fine lady moods'. At such times she could be arrogant and inconsiderate.

She had good reason to think that Harry Cust would ask for her hand in marriage. He was very much a 'Soul': A politician and editor of *The Pall Mall Gazette* during its short existence. As a man he was charming, amorous, witty, cynical and unscrupulous. In the event, his conduct towards the beautiful, intellectual but 'non-Soul' Miss Nina Welby-Gregory was such that Arthur Balfour insisted he married her instead of Pamela. He did so, with the worst possible grace. He neglected and humiliated her for most of his life thereafter, though she loved him faithfully until his early death at the age of 57. Pamela was devastated at the time of losing Harry, but it is very doubtful if a marriage would have been successful.

She now turned to one of brother George's friends, Edward Priaulx ('Eddie') Tennant, whom she married in 1895. He was to become Baron Glenconner. At first they lived in the family home in Peeblesshire, but later built a new manor at Wilsford near Amesbury. The house was designed by Detmar Blow, using traditional local materials in a very sensitive way.

The architect's Bohemian charm held great attraction for Pamela, as it had for her friend Violet Milford before her. Sir Edward Grey, later first Viscount Grey of Fallodon, was a close friend of the family. Two years after Eddie Tennant's early death in 1920, he became Pamela's second husband.

Pamela's early upbringing of her son Stephen was bizarre – she seems to have wished that he had been a girl. She herself died of a stroke in 1928.

The Staff

The staff existed not only to carry out the wide range of duties necessary to make the estate run smoothly, but also to reflect the status of the owner.

Written records provide basic facts about the numbers employed as indoor and outdoor staff, but only rarely does a picture emerge of their characters and lifestyle.

The agent for the estate was Edward Miles, whose parents were farmers. Perhaps the next most influential was William Mallett, a Gloucestershire man like his wife. They and their family (in 1891) of three sons and three daughters had Park Cottage converted for them by Percy, to whom he became indispensable as Estate Carpenter and later Clerk of Works. Percy selected him as Fire Brigade Captain, and when he was appointed Clerk of Works, he rode round the estate on a pony. After Percy's death he was even more influential as a fount of knowledge during George Wyndham's two years as Clouds' owner. He became very experienced in both design and execution of alterations, to both house and

William Mallett, Clerk of Works and Captain of the estate Fire Brigade.

for the estate generally. His wife was somewhat socially conscious of her husband's importance. He was a churchwarden, and as the responsibility for the fabric of the church rested with the appointment, he was, of course, well qualified. His experience and trusted position gave him the right to be consulted on all major projects; indeed he was quite ready to take issue with architects and to overrule them if he thought it necessary. He remained in harness until his death in 1923, serving Percy, George, Perf, Guy and Dick.

The Malletts' son William worked with his father. Ernie Mallett, who sang in the church choir for over 60 years, also learned his trade from his father. In World War I he served as a driver in France. Afterwards he set up his own business as carpenter, ironmonger and undertaker. He never married, though Miss Green, headmistress at West Knoyle and later a teacher at East Knoyle, was said to have been an unsuccessful suitor. Ernie was for many years a member of the East Knoyle, Semley and Sedgehill Branch of the British (now Royal British) Legion. The Malletts' grand-daughter, Mrs Mary Hall, who now lives in Warminster, has many memories of the village.

The central post of butler was occupied by William Icke from 1892,while his wife was housekeeper to two maiden ladies in the village. There is little direct evidence about him, apart from his formal speeches as chief of staff on family occasions, but the fact that the household ran so smoothly in coping with a constant influx of visitors indicates that he was on top of his important job and enjoyed the confidence of his master. His sitting room in the mansion commands splendid views of the gardens.

Mrs Simnett, the housekeeper, held an almost equally responsible position, taking over from Frances Vine when she retired. Mr Frank Barnes, headmaster from 1910 to 1948, used to call on her to take tea. Mr and Mrs Barnes looked after her in their house, 'Church Cottage', when she was ill. The cook (the Wyndhams did not employ a chef) was Mrs Wilks, with a staff of three kitchen maids. After the family moved to Clouds, they were joined by their head gardener from Wilbury, Henry ('Harry') Brown. Madeline planned the layout and contents of the gardens with him and took a keen, supportive

The garden staff at Clouds after Harry Brown's time, with the tools of their trade: Left to Right – A Street, Edward Jukes, Walter Fletcher, John Maidment, W Ford, Mr Lampard, James Fricker, F Coombes, C Strat, Frederick Littlecott, Ernest Carpenter.

interest. A great feature was the 2,500 rose plants, of which hybrid tea were the most prominent. The yew hedges were cut once a year, with some being trimmed into the shape of peacocks' tails. Magnolias were planted on the South front, with roses and myrtles in the border below. Upwards away from the mansion was the 'River Walk'. This was not a water feature but was so named because it wound like a river to the top. On each side were flowering shrubs. There were magnolias and spring bulbs, with mature cedars in the background. Towards the water tower was the tennis court, with its rose arch, behind which was the golf course.

Five of Madeline's grandchildren were killed in World War I, during the later part of which the Wyndham family made Clouds available as a convalescent home for wounded servicemen. During and after the War, Guy, his wife Minnie and their son Dick struggled to keep the estate solvent and in some sort of order. 'Bend Or' (the Duke of Westminster) took up a short lease of Clouds in 1924 to please them. He involved himself in village affairs: arranging outings for the schoolchildren and supporting the Scout Troop run by Mrs Neville, whose husband had succeeded Canon Milford as Rector in 1912.

The next tenants were the Dutchman Mr Adriaan Mosselman, his wife Nancy and their family. Mrs Winifred Hyde (née Stevens) lives in one of the

Clouds in 1995. Its life continues as a successful alcohol and drug dependency treatment centre.

houses built in 1911 by George Wyndham and William Mallett. Having been a nanny to the five Mosselman children, she can well remember Clouds as it was before Dick Wyndham embarked on the programme of sales which was to empty Clouds for ever of its Wyndham spirit.

The Milfords

The third prominent family were the Milfords, whose head (Robert Newman Milford) was Rector from 1866 to 1912, and thus in close contact with the village as a whole.

We also know a lot about them. Sources of information include: the *Western Gazette*, the Village Scrapbooks, the church magazine, published and unpublished family journals, diaries and reminiscences; together with memories still fresh in the minds of the oldest residents or handed down from their parents.[1] All of these contribute to a rich mosaic.

The picture is recognisable, even familiar, in some respects; in others it is light years away from life at the start of the 21st century.

Origins

Robert's grandfather was John Milford, a merchant of Exeter, who founded the City Bank there. His son, also named John, became senior partner and died at the age of 96. Like his father he was a great port drinker and would have been one of those to be offered a glass of claret at the Rectory table, where beer and wine became increasingly rare, except on special occasions. Robert's daughter Violet relates that if the favoured visitor accepted: 'one of the family would slip away from the dinner table, take the cellar key from father's drawer, and unlocking the door go down the stone steps to the cavernous cellar and bring up a bottle for the visitor's enjoyment'. Any wine undrunk would remain in the bottle which would be stood on its head in the corner for the next occasion. As Violet added, 'and very sour it probably was'!

Robert's mother was Eliza Neave, the daughter of a judge in the service of the East India Company. Robert was born in 1829 and after one or two false starts, was sent away to a boarding school attached to the Rectory at

Charlton Kings near Cheltenham. The school's teaching was poor and the establishment eventually failed. However, young Robert's memories of his journeys to and from school by coach prompted him to write a vivid account over 30 years later:

> Our journeys . . . were performed on top of the 'Exquisite Coach', which made the 110 miles with a quarter of an hour for dinner in ten hours. At Christmas-time, when the coach was loaded with boys' luggage and Christmas hampers, I have seen the coaches going down the hills full trot, swaying from side to side, and have often wondered that no accident ever happened to us. The red faces, weather-beaten, and also the unfailing brandy and water taken at every stage, of the coachman and guard, are still vividly before me, and the swiftness with which the four fresh horses were exchanged for the tired ones, only one and a half minutes being allowed. At all times of the night the horses were out in the road with their harness on as the coach drove up.
>
> At Bristol we used to look with wonder at the great turtle in a reservoir in the inn yard, alive and waiting to be turned into the turtle soup for which Bristol was famous. We had woollen comforters round our throats and small cloaks to our hips, but all that was allowed for the feet was a little straw, which if it rained or snowed added to our discomfort and cold. I have often wondered that we did not fall off the coach, as I remember we had to sit on the uncomfortable, uncushioned wooden seat with only one iron back-and-side rail, and our feet dangling over the coach-wheel. I often think how I used to nod, wake with a start, and find myself hanging on to the rail and all but fall off. And then the misery of the wintertime, of coming down in the coach! Often I have had to be lifted off, with feet so cold that I did not know when we were down on the ground.

Eventually, on his sixteenth birthday and after some other educational experiments, Robert was sent to Rugby School. His age placed him fairly high up the school, but the lack of an adequate grounding in Latin and Greek meant that much of the teaching went over his head. Three years later he entered Balliol College, Oxford, where, again, his academic career was undistinguished.

He took a pass degree in 1851, but (as his grandson put it) 'he was given the very back-handed compliment of honorary fourth class honours'. A year later, as was usual for sons in wealthy families, he made the Grand Tour. He left Liverpool in April 'and called at Constantinople, Smyrna, Syracuse, Athens, Corfu, Malta and Italy, reaching home in November'.

The time had come to embark on a career. He began to attend Divinity lectures in Oxford and early in 1853 decided to read for Holy Orders. Seeking advice on what should be his first post after ordination, he consulted Bishop George Sumner. Bishop George held the diocese of Guildford, carved out of part of the vast see of Winchester – held by his father Bishop Charles Sumner. The Sumner family home was Farnham Castle, where by 1853 Emily Sumner was hostess, having taken up the responsibility when her mother died four years earlier. Robert's visit was to shape the rest of his life, for not only was he steered towards a curate's vacancy in Stockwell, south London, but he met his future wife. As Robert put it in his memoirs: 'the last day of June 1853 I went to Farnham Castle as a candidate for ordination, little thinking that by God's great goodness I was to find there a dear father [Bishop Charles] a loving wife, and a happy home'. 'She was very much sought after and might often before have married, but she chose the life of a clergyman's wife'.

Coming to Knoyle

Robert was ordained deacon at the end of July 1853 – ordination training seems to have been less rigorous or at least less lengthy in those days – and began work at Stockwell. The next year Robert and Emily were married. Eleven years later the parish of East Knoyle in Salisbury diocese fell vacant. It was the richest living in the gift of Bishop Charles, whose predecessors as Bishops of Winchester had been lords of the manor of East or Bishop's Knoyle since the 13th century. In technical terms, they held the 'advowson', the right as patrons to appoint the Rector. This sort of nepotism would create a stir nowadays, but would not have caused much comment at that time. Fortunately for Knoyle, Robert had given ample proof of his suitability in his clerical career so far and was well qualified for the post – in his family he was regarded as 'energetic and a good, simple preacher'. In addition to his stipend as Rector, Robert had ample financial resources from his family and was able to live in comfortable style, though without parading his wealth.

The Rectory

The Rectory to which the Milford family moved was in two parts. The older was a surviving portion of the mediaeval glebe house dating from the 15th century. This was where Sir Christopher Wren's family had lived.

In 1799, when the Rev John Ogle was Rector, a large new Georgian house had been built at the eastern end. At that time the road from the village centre to Holloway ran along the southern side of the house. Although the term 'nimby' (Not In My Back Yard) had not been invented, it seems to describe the Rector's attitude precisely. He obtained permission to divert the highway in a semicircle away from the house, created a boundary wall and laid out a garden falling away from the new South front with its five bays.

The dovecote which had caused Sir Christopher Wren's father such problems in 1636 was still in existence and the building remains today.

While generally pleased with the estate and its amenities, Robert Milford found the provision for horses inadequate. Looking round the glebe land his gaze lighted with a jaundiced eye on the tithe barn opposite the church. Until 1844, the Rectors' tithes had been stored there in kind, but when these were commuted to money payments it no longer served its original purpose. In Robert's application to the Tithe Commissioners he wrote that it had 'been rendered useless'. Along with a carthouse, lumber shed and cowstall nearby, he sought permission to demolish the lot, sell the materials and use the proceeds. Along with £50 paid by the previous Rector in dilapidations when he left, Robert intended to build a new range of buildings in the Rectory grounds to provide stabling for four horses, together with a harness room and a coach house.

The Commissioners' enquiries were thorough, but in the end they gave authority for the changes in 1868. The stabling was duly built, but the barn seems to have been reprieved. It lasted another 93 years until burnt down in a careless accident in 1961.

Robert Milford, Rector and Family Man

R obert, as Rector and head of the family believed firmly in God, the Church of England and the established social order; within which every individual should be encouraged to play a positive part. Emily, his wife, echoed these beliefs, including the importance of recognising social standing. She was thought by some villagers to be far too 'high and mighty'. She apparently expected the village women and girls to curtsy on meeting any of her family; while men and boys should bow and touch their forelocks.[2]

Her daughter Violet was, by contrast, very much at ease with everyone in the village and happy to work with others for village causes. However, in her early years, she accepted the laid down social distinction as quite natural. She recalled with some amusement how one older village woman so far forgot herself in a moment of excitement as to clasp her waist. She also noted that at a concert in which she was performing at Romsey in 1892: 'Some tradesmen from the town helped sing – one had an excellent bass voice. They had supper with us afterwards'.

Throughout the whole of his forty-six years as Rector, he applied his energies to the spiritual and material wellbeing of his parishioners. He was tireless in promoting action to make his perception of their needs a reality. With the assistance of a succession of curates, he provided a full range of mainstream Church of England services that appealed to a broad cross-section of the community.

He produced and edited a parish magazine for over a quarter of a century which gave details of parish services and wider church activities such as overseas missions. It also gave a revealing insight into social causes of which he approved, forthright condemnation of moral failings in personal, village or national life, village sport (especially cricket but also football), local and national events.

He had no leanings towards Roman Catholicism. Indeed, in one article on church history he came close to explaining the English Reformation solely as an inevitable consequence of abuses by the Church of Rome; without even passing reference to the family planning and personal ambitions of Henry VIII!

'Dissenters', as he called them, fared little better. He did not go as far as one of his predecessors who bought an existing chapel building in the village and promptly closed it down. However, his contacts with the Congregational minister responsible for the nonconformist British School until its closure in 1881 were frostily minimal. There was a third village church institution in the Primitive Methodists, whose chapel at the Green had been built in 1843.

Despite his unshakeable faith in Anglican values, the need for expression of village unity could when necessary take precedence. The death of Queen Victoria in 1901 was one such an occasion. On 2nd February there was a memorial service in the Parish Church, with every seat filled. Robert recorded that, 'It was a wonderful sight . . . that mourning multitude – Church and Chapel people all together at one in mourning for the dear good Queen'. The service was 'touching, simple and beautiful', and both beforehand and afterwards, 'a beautiful muffled peal was rung, five of the bells being muffled on both sides, and the sixth (the tenor) ringing out clear as a knell'.

When the Church of England 'National' school (roughly where the bus shelter is now) became too small for its purpose after the passing of the 1870 Education Act, the Rector fought hard to retain the right to give religious instruction in accordance with Church of England doctrine. After the 'British' school closed, its 40 or 50 children were transferred to the single village school on its new site in Church Road. These children were excused from the Religious

Education classes then held at the end of Friday morning lessons, but the subject remained a contentious one for many years.

From about 1848 Mr John Tanswell had been headmaster. He was assisted by Miss Brockway until her retirement in 1871 and then by Miss Minns. The latter is recorded as being 'very sound' in teaching needlework, but being 'all of a twitter' on examination days.

John Tanswell was much respected throughout his 44 years as headmaster. The Rector's close interest in the workings of the school must have been somewhat of a mixed blessing at times; but there seems to have been a good measure of mutual appreciation between the headmaster, the Rector and his family. He was also well supported by old Mrs Seymour of Knoyle House until her death in 1869, and then by her son Alfred and his wife. The Wyndhams also took a benevolent, practical interest.

The pay of a headmaster was meagre. Mr Tanswell supplemented it by playing the organ in church, as well as by giving private tuition to the Milford children in grammar and arithmetic.

There is, by coincidence, a direct link between the school's first headmaster in his black tail coat bound with braid and the last headmaster. He was also called John Tanswell, and was well respected. He died shortly after the school was closed in 1984.

John Tanswell was succeeded by Miss Woodcock, who was also well regarded by the Rector, the village and her pupils. When she left after 18 years service to be married, her replacement was the 26-year-old Mr Frank Barnes, a native of Salisbury but previously an assistant master in Walthamstow. He, too, seems to have made a good start in the Rector's eyes, with his establishment of a voluntary twice-weekly night school for young men and boys, which started with a register of 30.

The Family

The Milford family was a stable and well ordered one. The first five children were born within seven years of each other, before Robert and Emily came to Knoyle. There was then an eight year gap until Violet was born, followed by Henry who died in infancy, and finally Humphrey five years later.

None of the daughters went to school, but were put in the care of a succession of governesses. In Violet's time, Miss Slaughter was followed by Fräulein Marie Margarethe Streiff. 'Fräulein' , as she was known, was a pretty and impulsive Swiss girl who made time in the schoolroom interesting or

A Milford family wedding at Shipton under Wychwood, Oxfordshire, in August 1894. Theodore married Elsbeth Barter. The Rector, then aged 65, bought nearby Yockleton Hall preparatory school for them, but with only about 12 boys it failed after a few years. Theodore was more successful as a sportsman. A competent cricketer and soccer player, he was once a runner-up in the All England Tennis Championships at Wimbledon.

grim according to her moods. She and Humphrey did not seem to get on, though Violet's relationship with her was much better. When schoolwork restarted after Christmas 1882, and Violet's birthday on Boxing Day, Fräulein apologised to her for having been impatient and, 'hoped that they would get on better in the next term'. Violet recognised this gratefully for what it was – an unusual and caring gesture from an adult to a child pupil in those days.

When Fräulein left and Humphrey went four miles away to school in Fonthill, Violet's sisters took over the task of educating her and were very thorough about it. Eleanor ('Ella') soon got married, so the work was then left almost entirely in the hands of her younger sister Marion ('Mai'). At this point Beatrice Milford dutifully returned from her job as a social worker in Stepney to help in the parish. She loved the village people, but relations with her much loved parents could be strained at times – and Mai, though five years her junior, was a very strong character.

By the time that Violet could remember, she regarded her parents as already 'elderly people': Robert was nearing 50 and his wife two or three years younger. In his youth he had been a keen cricketer, and encouraged his sons to play in the village team and elsewhere. The village club was refounded in 1896 and given Seymour land at Summerleaze to play on; which had been newly relaid 'with the advice of a professional'. Nor was sport restricted to the men. Violet herself was no mean golfer and could meet the men on equal terms on the Wyndham's nine hole golf course above The Green. On at least one occasion Robert himself had a round with his daughter.

Both Robert and Emily were kind people who cared about their children, giving them thoughtful little gifts as well as treats from time to time, which were always appreciated. Ground rules of behaviour seem to have been accepted by all concerned, and both Violet and Humphrey were given considerable freedom of action.

When grandchildren visited in Robert's later years, he was seen as:

> already venerable, always kind but somewhat distant. He occasionally took part in a gentle game of golf-croquet, swinging his mallet between his legs, in an unorthodox manner, which his family called 'grandfather-wise'. He walked slowly round the village, visiting, and preached with an impressive voice on Sundays.

Emily, by contrast, was:

> small, active and bustling, with a lace cap and a silk or velvet skirt, and a 'chatelaine' at her waist with jangling keys and scissors. She sat very upright in a small upholstered chair, and was a great one for playing games, Halma, Colorito or Backgammon, in which she enjoyed banging the cup with the dice on a little mat in the shiny inlaid board.

Although their family gave Robert and Emily great cause for contentment, a long shadow was cast in 1896. Seymour Milford, named after the Seymours of Knoyle House, gave early promise by winning the solo singing prize at Haileybury. After his voice broke it deepened into a very fine baritone. When he left Haileybury, he went up to Oxford University, then on to the Royal College of Music to study music and singing. An operation on his tonsils ruined the tone of his singing voice for a while. A severe bout of influenza followed, which left him very depressed. A sea voyage to Australia was suggested as a cure; but since clinical depression was not as well understood then as it is now, no special precautions were taken. Tragically, one day, he disappeared from the ship. The whole family was devastated, going into deep and extended mourning.

A Day at The Rectory

The family's day started with prayers before breakfast. The gong was rung at half past eight each morning. Robert would be seated at one end of the table, with the Bible open in front of him and a pile of prayer books alongside. Emily would be close to the copper urn with its methylated spirit lamp flickering underneath. The bell would then be rung to summon the maids who 'trooped in to sit on a form covered with red baize at the other end of the room in front of the oak sideboard'. The maids followed the lesson in their Bibles. Prayers over, the red baize form 'was whisked away' and the bustle of the day began. When Violet was young, it was the practice to have a chapter from the Bible read verse and verse about by those present.

Robert would take a stroll in the garden and then retire to his cold study to read, or engage in visiting and other parish business. Emily would give orders for dinner, visit the sick and needy or write letters at the upright bureau by the fire in the drawing room. With national health and social services a thing of the future, the Rector and members of his family kept a caring eye out for those needing help and did their best to see that assistance, financial or otherwise reached those who deserved it.

Usually, their efforts were successful, but on one occasion they led to an appearance in court. The Rector, when visiting the Moxham family who worked on the farm for George Bridwell at Friar's Hayes, found them quite ill with a fever, so he notified Dr McElpatrick. The doctor treated the patients and then sent the Rector a bill for 15 Guineas (£15.75) a sizeable sum in those days. The Rector 'naturally refused to pay', so the matter had to be resolved in the County Court on 17th March 1893. The family were convinced that the Judge had summed up entirely in the Rector's favour, but the jury felt otherwise. Although Violet, the three sons who were present and the curate Mr Williams were all incensed at the outcome, the Rector accepted the verdict calmly without rancour.

The evenings would be times for making music, at which many of the family were proficient, or for playing games. These included 'Spoof', a card game, also 'Cassino' – in which one tried to get rid of all one's cards, which had to be combined to make 11 and carried various values.

Family Social Life

The family's social life was conducted at a number of levels. The Rector played his part in the clerical affairs of the Salisbury diocese, and through his wife's family with Winchester diocese also.

There was frequent social contact on both a personal and parish level with both the Wyndham and Seymour families. Violet was good friends with Jane Seymour from Knoyle House. Pamela Wyndham was also a frequent companion who could be very good company when she so chose. At other times, when she was in what Violet described as one of her 'fine lady' moods, things were different. One occasion when both had gone to a Primrose League meeting at Sedgehill, a couple of miles away, Pamela ordered her own coachman to drive home on the unspoken assumption that the Rectory coachman would take her back as well.

The Milford social circle included the Morrisons of Fonthill. Margaret Thatcher put forward a noted descendant, M.P. and long time Chairman of the Conservative '1922 Committee' for a hereditary peerage and he became Lord Margadale. Lady Stalbridge at Motcombe and later Knoyle House was a particular favourite, but her family suffered severe financial losses connected with Lord Sudeley.

Family visits to London with the Bradby family provided an opportunity to visit the theatre, and there was also a memorable holiday in Snowdonia. The usual method of travel for long journeys was by train from Semley station three miles away. The Milfords kept three horses and a pony; so both the open carriage and the pony cart were a common sight in the neighbourhood.

Robert's curates brought relief to the Rector's workload, but it was difficult to find ones who met his needs. If they were young and energetic, the parish of some 900 generally well ordered souls did not provide much of a challenge; but old or sick men were no good either.

His first choice was a lively Irishman, who took Violet out riding and organised skating expeditions in the winter. His particular fancy was Ella, who seems to have had over half a dozen proposals of marriage. The curate is recorded as doing ' his Irish best' to win her affections away from her fiancé, Hermann David, but failed. Soon after she married Hermann the curate left and went to work in a mining village. The only one to find real favour with the Rector was the Welshman, Mr Griffith Williams. Robert built a house for him at The Green which he named 'Parson's Paddock'. Williams was appointed to a living of his own after a number of years.

The most extraordinary holder of the office was Jewish and came from Romania. His English was strongly accented and on his birthday he said that he used to receive curses instead of presents and good wishes from his relatives! No assessment of his worth from any source outside the Milford family is recorded. However, for them his 'crowning offence was to write a letter to Beatrice when her parents were away, proposing marriage'.

Courtship and marriage were subjects of genuinely supportive interest to all the younger generation. Violet herself became greatly attracted to the young architect Detmar Blow. Blow was a pupil of the eminent Philip Webb, who was commissioned by Percy Wyndham to design and superintend the construction of the new Clouds House in the 1880s and its rebuilding after the great fire of 1889.

Blow became a regular guest of the Wyndhams from 1892. However, his contact with the Milfords was mainly in connection with the restoration of St. Mary's church tower. With his rather long curly hair and loose homespun suit, he was a romantic figure who made, perhaps unconsciously, a big impression on the ladies. He and Violet shared common interests in making music and in philosophical discussion. Although all the Milford ladies enjoyed his company and Emily was pleased to invite him round, the Rector was less enthusiastic.

Blow lodged with the Widow Snook in Underhill but left the village when the tower project had been completed. He returned from time to time as a guest of the Wyndhams, executing a number of commissions for the family, including their memorial in the new churchyard opposite the Rectory. He took no steps to deepen his relationship with Violet; eventually marrying Winifred Tollemache some 18 years later, who was the granddaughter of Lord Tollemache of Helmingham Hall in Suffolk.

Violet's own marriage was not to be long delayed. The Milfords in Knoyle and the Bradbys in London had exchanged visits since Violet's childhood. During the first summer after Dr Bradby's death in December 1892, the family had come down to stay at a cottage in Knoyle belonging to the Rectory. The longstanding acquaintance between Violet and Henry Christopher (known as 'Kit') quietly ripened into something more. After just a fortnight, he proposed to her at the ornamental sundial in the Rectory garden and was accepted.

The engagement was meant to be a secret at first. But on a drive in the brake with the coachman Mike Nisbeck to picnic at Stonehenge they sat together; and when Kit went off on a cricket tour the secret was soon out.

The wedding at Knoyle the next April was memorable in more ways than one. There was a violent thunderstorm, so that the lower part of the church became flooded. Violet later wrote that while standing at the altar steps she could see the lightning zigzagging down through what was then the plain glass of the east window. The bridesmaids had to be lifted out of church into the waiting carriage for the short drive to the Rectory.

As the bride and groom left the church, 20 little girls from the Girls' Friendly Society strewed flowers in their path. They then passed under an arch of evergreens over the entrance to the churchyard with the initials V.A.M.

and H.C.B. on a board. The carriage later drove through another arch put up over the Rectory gates.

The weather cleared up. Photographs were taken, presents were admired, tea was served in the school and General Pitt-Rivers' Band (not the East Knoyle Village Band) played on the lawn until a second heavy storm came on.

The new Mrs Bradby must have been a decided asset to her schoolmaster husband, who later became a housemaster at Rugby School. However, at first they lived 'in small houses with small gardens and a small income'. Although her parents were by no means poor, she was taught to appreciate the need for thrift and self-sufficiency. She was a keen, sympathetic but not uncritical observer of life around her and ready to lend a hand in all sorts of good causes. Before her marriage she helped in the village school from time to time and taught young children (whom she often referred to as 'chicks') in Sunday School. Unpaid social work was an important part of Rectory life, especially visiting the sick and disadvantaged. She would do what she could for the young widow when, as frequently happened, the husband died leaving a large family.

One of the old ladies on Violet's visiting list in 1893 was Ann Wass, born in 1802. They seem to have got on well; for Violet remembered her saying to the young visitor 71 years her junior: 'I do like to look at you, you are so beautiful'.

At the 1881 Census, Ann had been classed as 'a pauper' lodging with George Ford, a general labourer, his wife (Also Ann) and their three children at 35 Milton, next to the Dairy House. Only a few months afterwards, George died; but Ann remained with his widow until her death twelve years later. Ann was then sent away and placed in the Workhouse at Mere, 'The Mere Union', five miles distant. Emily Milford and Violet drove out to see her there but, 'She seemed so sad, poor old dear'. This was not surprising, for she had been uprooted from the village which had been her home for 92 years – and few of her neighbours would have been able to make the journey out to visit her. As the Committee writing *The Story of Mere* has noted: 'Conditions inside the workhouse were intended to be as unattractive as possible to deter any but the destitute . . . the result was a drab, grudging and soulless institution'.[3] The Union, situated in Castle Street, was closed in 1931, when all the patients were transferred to Tisbury. Most of the buildings were pulled down but a little remains on and behind the Castle Hill Garage.[4]

Although, then as now, East Knoyle was a small village with a population of under a thousand, it would be wrong to think of ladies in Violet's position as being culturally deprived. She was familiar with the London theatre, while locally she sang in choral concerts and was an accomplished musician. Her particular love was the violin. She started lessons at the age of 13 with Alfred Foley at the music shop in New Canal, Salisbury. Five years later, she studied under Mr Gompertz in London at his lodgings off Baker Street. He was a hard taskmaster. However he found that she was diligent and had been well grounded, and recommended that she should study at the Royal College of Music. This did not come about, but she continued to play regularly for over 40 years.

She was proficient in French, German and Italian. She enjoyed sketching. She designed and executed a beautiful altar cloth for the Church which was first used on Easter Sunday 1893. Another activity was writing; for Violet was the author of many delightful children's books. She also wrote 'A Family Chronicle' to record a way of life in her youth which she recognised as very different from conditions at the time of writing – during World War II. This was printed for private circulation in 1942 and is a treasure house of careful observation and perceptive comment which brings the people and events of her youth to life.

Politics and National Events

The Milford family, like their Wyndham neighbours, were Conservatives in politics. Indeed, when Sir Thomas Grove was elected as a Liberal for the South Wiltshire division, Violet put her diary 'into mourning for the day' by drawing a black ink line all around it. 'Old Gladstone' as she called him and his Irish Home Rule Bill of 1893 got short shrift also. When Violet's husband Kit mentioned to Mike Nisbeck the coachman 'I'm a Radical, you know Mike', he could only gasp and reply 'Never, Sir!'

Conservative Party values were fostered in the Primrose League, with the Hon. Percy Wyndham being 'Ruling Councillor' of its 'Knoyle Vale Habitation'. Concerts for the village, to which the Milford family made significant contributions and which were very popular, would include a few minutes talk on political topics by Mr Wyndham, which always seem to have been enthusiastically received.

The family took a keen interest in national and royal events, though with a critical and often discerning eye. When the Imperial Institute in South Kensington was opened in 1893, Mai and Violet went up to town to see something of the procession led by the Prince of Wales (later Edward VII), Prince George, Princess Mary and the Duchess of Teck. Violet commented that the engagement of Prince George and Mary of Teck (later to become George V and Queen Mary) was, 'horrid, one time or another she must be marrying lovelessly.' This was in fact a view shared by quite a number of people in the country.

By 1887, the year of her Golden Jubilee, Queen Victoria's popularity was rising, as she gradually emerged from her strict self-imposed seclusion after the early death of her beloved Albert. Her purity of life, simple home tastes, and her surprising ability to know what the ordinary people were thinking were becoming more appreciated. Added to this was a sense of pride in the worldwide extent of her British and Indian Empires. In short, Britain was ready to celebrate. National rejoicings were matched in cities, towns and villages throughout the land.

After a further ten years, Britain, India, the Dominions and Colonies once more set to with a will to mark the 60 years of her 'Longest and Most Glorious Reign'. In Knoyle, the programme of celebration was a full one. On the Sunday beforehand, there were special services in the parish church. Diamond Jubilee Day, Tuesday the 22nd of June began with a cloudy sky but during the morning this gave way to fine 'royal weather'. The church bells rang out at 7.30 a.m. and at intervals throughout the day. A new Union Jack flew from the church tower and there were also flags flying from many houses in the village.

At 3.45 p.m., the first of about 750 teas (cake, bun, bread and butter for the children, 'a substantial meat tea' for those over 15) was served at the school by Stewards, most of the Sports Committee and a tireless Ladies' Committee. The school and its playground were beautifully decorated. Those waiting were entertained by the village band or danced on the Rectory lawn. The school children were resplendent in red white and blue Japanese paper sashes given them by the Rector and Mrs Milford.

Punctually at 6 p.m. a procession formed up and moved to Windmill Hill marching behind the band. There they found most of the rest of the village waiting. A full programme of athletic sports for both adults and children was followed by a firework display master-minded by the curate, Mr Mallet the Clouds estate carpenter and Mr Bazley.

At 11 p.m. the celebrations came to an end with the band playing for the full-throated singing of all three verses of the National Anthem; including the combative second verse which is rarely heard nowadays:

O Lord our God arise   Frustrate their knavish tricks;
Scatter our enemies   On Thee our hopes we fix;
And make them fall;   God save us all.
Confound their politics,

Church Festivals

These were celebrated much as now, with the church specially decorated for Easter, Harvest Festival and Christmas. Up until 1752 the Church's Patronal Festival of St. Mary took place in conjunction with Knoyle Feast. However, when the calendar was corrected to take up an error of eleven days the Feast remained on its old date, which was the first Monday after 19th September.

The Village Scrapbooks, compiled by the Women's Institute in the 1950s, record the scene:

> The local hounds 'The South & West Wilts' always met on the Windmill Hill in the morning and the villagers followed them on foot. Meanwhile there was a public luncheon at the *Fox & Hounds*, held in the Coach House, where one could fortify oneself with bread and cheese and beer, as the Inn remained open all day. The local (East Knoyle) brass band was in attendance all day and to add to the amusement there were roundabouts, swings and various stalls. A quoits match was held on the Green and Barney Sharp from Gillingham always came with his donkey and cart, from which he sold all kinds of nuts. Unfortunately with the passing of time nearly all these functions have died out. The hounds usually meet on this day, but this is not always possible owing to late harvests. A parish social is now held in the Village Hall.

Knoyle Feast is now only a memory, though it is pictured on the fine mural in the Village Hall. This was commissioned by Miss Elizabeth Glen-Coats in 1985, executed by Ronald Homes, and is reproduced on the cover of this book.

Club Day

In the days before national public health and social service provision, responsibility for relief rested with the parish and perhaps the squire or Rector – and what individuals and groups could do for themselves.

In Knoyle in 1810, during the wars with Napoleon, there was established 'The Union Society'. This had as its object 'raising by contributions, a fund for the relief of its members in sickness, and for their mutual benefit, and to impose and inflict certain fines on the several members who shall offend against the rules, orders and regulations, and for other good causes, intents and purposes.' The Society met at the *Black Horse Inn* (now Black Horse House) every six weeks.

Benefits were quite substantial for the period. First class members, for instance, paid 6s. (30p) every six weeks; but when ill would receive 9s. (45p) a week for the first eight weeks, then 4s. 6d. (22.5p)a week for the next eight weeks, then 2s. 3d. (11.5p) a week until recovery. Money was paid on the death of a member or his wife towards funeral expenses.

Club Day about 1910, when the club celebrated its centenary. Note the band, the two banners, and the members with their poles.

Precautions were taken against fraud. No money was forthcoming for those with venereal disease, those guilty of murder or theft, or those who enlisted in Her Majesty's Service (!). Disorder at meetings was punished by fines.[5]

The great Club Day was held on the first Thursday after Whitsun, with all the village keen to be present – girls in domestic service elsewhere would try to get the day off to come. The roll would be called in the Club Room in time to attend church at 11 a.m. Absence without good causes carried a fine of 5s. (25p). Every pew would be filled and 'the singing drowned the organ'. According to the Village Scrapbook, each member on leaving was given a shilling (5p) – though the Rules talk of imposing a shilling fine for not remaining throughout the service. Either way, an encouragement to be present.

After the service, a procession formed up behind the Village Band. There were two crimson silk banners – one with a picture of the Good Samaritan and his donkey on it and gold tassels. The four stewards held coloured poles with streamers fluttering from the top. The rest of the members each had a coloured pole with a round top. Both members and supporters wore rosettes in the club colours of red, white and blue made of 'sarsnet' (a fine, thin, soft silk used for ribbon).

The assembly then proceeded the two or three hundred yards to the Rectory porch. The band played a few tunes and the Rector then headed the march back to the school for the festival dinner. Despite the Rules being very harsh on misbehaviour, one or two members might by now be somewhat merry with drink. One in particular used to take up position by the school gate and barrack the members going in for their meal. In an interview with the late Mr Alfred ('Alfie') Tanswell who witnessed Club Days as a child he was asked what the Rector thought of such goings-on. 'No, he didn't like it', Alfie replied, 'but he had to put up with it, didn't he?'

An enormous meal was then consumed, with rounds of beef, cheese and much beer; for which each member paid 2s. 6d. (12.5p). At about three o'clock brass band playing and dancing took place on the Rectory lawn, including a traditional dance called 'Bricks and mortar' performed to a cheerful but monotonous tune.

Then it was off behind the band to neighbouring villages, followed by a return to the school for cheese, more beer and dancing until 10 o'clock. For those unable to cope with making their own way home, it is said that wagons were discreetly placed in the yard opposite the school, into which members would be quietly lifted to sleep it off. The story is told of one Sedgehill man who fell into a ditch on his way home and remained there for three days!

The Club reached its centenary successfully, but was not revived after World War I, and was formally wound up in 1929.

Drunkenness

As Queen Victoria's reign progressed, the nation's conscience was increasingly pricked by the evidence of families becoming wretched and destitute through excessive drinking, mainly by the male wage earners.

Temperance movements sprang up to combat the sort of depravity portrayed by Charles Dickens. Periodical magazines like *The Light of Day* sought to provide 'improving' yet readable stories to interest both old and young, with sensible recipes and household hints to maintain interest.

In Knoyle *The Light of Day* was widely read; but the main focus was on the Church of England Temperance Society or C.E.T.S. There were three classes of membership: Juniors, Non Total Abstainers and those who signed a pledge not to drink alcohol at all. Visiting speakers regularly came to village C.E.T.S. meetings to convince their audiences of the evils of alcohol, to recruit new members and to spur on those already within the fold. Some, like Sergeant Major Grindle of the Coldstream Guards who used to appear in full uniform, were highly regarded; but others were less effective.

The Rector appreciated that exhortation on its own would not be enough. He recognised that sobriety should still be fun. Concerts and entertainments were put together, much enjoyed and well attended. In the summer there were outings, usually by train, which made membership something special.

The junior arm of the C.E.T.S. was the Band of Hope, from which members would progress to the Society itself. The first lines of its theme song ran: 'There's a little public house that everyone can close; and that's the little public house that's underneath your nose'. Her mother used to recite this reassuring jingle to Violet, but sometimes reality would intrude. When the two were about to board a train for London they saw a person apparently swigging alcohol and mother saying a bit too firmly 'Milk, my dear, milk' – it seems that Violet was not taken in!

The Girls' Friendly Society

Another organisation for young people was the Girls' Friendly Society of which the South Wilts Branch had a thriving section in the village. The objects of the Society were to band together ladies (as associates), girls and young women for mutual help (religious and secular) for sympathy and prayer; encouraging purity of life, dutifulness to parents, faithfulness to employers, and thrift. No girl who did not bear a virtuous character could be admitted and if 'such character be lost, the Member to forfeit her Card'. Despite this somewhat stern agenda, meetings and the annual Branch Summer Festival were well attended. In 1888, for example, 14 members drove to Old Wardour Castle for the Festival; and there was a list of 21 younger girls waiting to join. The official accounts printed in the Parish Magazine may have sometimes been a little highly coloured however, for Violet recalls an outing to Sherborne

The East Knoyle orchestra at the Rectory door about 1905, under the direction of Marion 'Mai' Milford. Those pictured here became proficient and included four members of the Littlecott family: Ernest (clarinet), Walter ('cello), Frank (violin) and Edward (cornet). Marion is recorded as 'cramming the schoolroom' with budding musicians who 'blew and scraped away in happy din, while she coached them and conducted at the piano'.

– one of what the village would call 'feasts and gaylers' which involved a visit to King Alfred's tower at Stourton. She later wrote how:

> The party drove the nine miles each way in waggons. The waggon either crawled along at a snail's pace, or else jolted you up and down agonizingly when the horses broke into a trot. For boredom, driving nine miles in a waggon is only equalled by a G.F.S. festival in a barge drawn by a horse which I later on endured at Rugby.

The Staff

In addition to the children's governess and the cook there were: Five indoor maids, the coachman, a head gardener, under gardener and two boys, and until the Rector gave up dairying, a cowman. There was also Mrs Ann Maidment, a widow who lived nearby in Church Rails but spent much time in the Rectory working as a dressmaker and needlewoman – at which she was very skilled.

Perhaps the linchpin of the establishment was Michael Nisbeck, a widow's son from the nearby village of Fonthill Gifford. In the 1890s he was in his thirties; a handsome quick-tempered man with a gift for apt phrases. Although perhaps too highly strung too be ideal for managing horses, he drove the two bays along at a rattling pace.

There were two carriages, the big one being a landau with a removable top. In summer he wore a very smart outfit of a light blue cloth livery coat with crested gilt buttons, top boots and a top hat. He was fiercely loyal to the Rector and his wife, but did not take kindly to any attempt by the daughters in particular to order him about.

Seymour and Violet, among the younger members of the family, were sometimes permitted to drive – usually without incident. On one occasion however, when out without Mike, Seymour turned Phyllis the mare too sharply at the top of Church Rails – still a bit of a hazard for a car 110 years later. The carriage mounted the steep bank, Phyllis would not back and the vehicle slowly turned over. Mike was sent for, the outfit turned right way up, Phyllis unharmed and the passengers' grazes quickly bound up. Mike's reactions are not recorded.

On another occasion Mai and Violet took 'Hughie' (the Hon. Hugh Grosvenor, eleven year old son of Lord and Lady Stalbridge from Knoyle House) out for a ride on Duke, with Mai holding a leading rein. Suddenly, the horse shied, kicked Hugh off, broke the leading rein, galloped away and refused to be caught 'jumping about in a most naughty way'. Order was eventually restored and George Garrett, a farm labourer who lived near the Rectory in Church Road being asked to ride Duke for a while to tire him, which he did. Then, in the best equestrian tradition, a shaken but otherwise unhurt Hugh was made to remount and the ride continued from Underhill to the Green and back to the stables, a distance of about a mile. The next day, Hugh was made to ride Duke again; which he achieved without mishap, but without much enjoyment either.

Mike was a keen cricketer who rose to captain the Knoyle team for a while. His batting averages were not particularly high, but he had a reputation as a demon underarm bowler. On Sundays he sang bass in the church choir. He lived with his wife and nine children in a glebe cottage in Holloway next to the Rectory. All the children survived into adulthood.

Mike's neighbours included the Tuck family. Eli Tuck, originally from Symondsbury near Bridport, was head gardener. He had a jutting brown beard which made him look like a Shakespearian actor. He was, apparently, unable to read or write, but he was certainly a first rate gardener. He was also a great talker and his conversation would pursue one down the garden path long after one walked away at the end of a chat with him. He personally superintended the lawn mowing, and in the summer it was a common sight to see him pushing the mowing machine along the narrow grass paths which wound in and out of the flower beds filled with geraniums and verbenas. The rest of the motive power was provided by one of the two gardener's boys pulling at the front. An unloved feature of the garden at one time was a monkey puzzle tree reckoned to disfigure the slope of the lawn. One night, someone ringed the bark so that it died, but neither Eli nor anyone else seemed to have the slightest idea who might have done it.

In later years Edward Garrett was the under gardener , with a part time job as sexton for the church. He was married to Ellen, head housemaid and later cook. They had a little boy called Reggie who was a favourite with all the household. When the Rector retired, Edward and Ellen went with them to Bournemouth, but sadly Reggie died there shortly afterwards.

Finally, there was the cowman, whose name was Woodley. With a mild, long face framed in brown whiskers, he looked like a character from one of Thomas Hardy's Wessex novels. His charges were rather prone to succumb to unidentified disorders; but whether this was due to lack of skill or not, he surely did not deserve to be on the receiving end of the Rector's experiment with silage. The silage pit was lined with cement and filled with wet grass which was battened down with heavy lids. The resulting slimy mass was fed to the cows, who loved it; but the cowman left a trail of strong, sour smell wherever he went – which was almost impossible to get rid of, and must have interfered with his social life.

The Last Years

In 1896, Robert's worth was officially recognised by being created a Canon of Salisbury cathedral. On their Golden Wedding in 1904, the family gathered round to celebrate and the parish presented them with a handsome silver-gilt bowl.

After 46 years of faithful service, Robert and Emily retired to live in Richmond Gardens in Bournemouth, when Robert was 83. In a characteristic gesture, Robert refused the pension to which he was entitled from the living saying: 'I have had a good income for many years and I do not feel it right to take anything more'.

21 June 1913. Canon Milford's funeral passing the school. His high church successor, the Rev William Neville (in biretta) follows the choir who are singing a hymn unaccompanied. The headmaster, Mr Frank Barnes, and his assistant pay their respects beside the Union flag at half mast.

He died on the 18th June 1913, and was buried at Knoyle. His funeral was a striking sight. A long procession of family, villagers and friends wound its way from the church past the school, where the teachers stood in silent tribute with the flag at half mast. A hymn was sung unaccompanied and his body buried in the new churchyard. His widow survived him for 13 years and was buried alongside her husband in the shade of an old lime tree just over the road from the Rectory.

A Retrospect

Robert Milford was a man of his time. He saw the birth of the modern age, tackling its problems with vigour and determination. In a period when public education was only slowly expanding and national social services as we know them were rudimentary; he provided stability and moral support, both to his family and all his parishioners.

With his death, an era was coming to an end. The 'Great War' was to begin the next year.

Work and Play

Both at the time of the 1841 Census and again 50 years later, agriculture was the main occupation; with work for the three big houses and general labouring not far behind. There was also a wide spread of shops and services.

The list below, culled from the 1891 Census by Mr R.W. ('Mick') Mickleburgh illustrates this very well: In a population of 887 (much the same as today's) there were 104 'scholars' not all itemised, with 241 of the children aged 12 and under. The Wyndham family and their houseguests are not included.

Under 'Occupations' we have:

Agricultural labourer 57	Engine driver 1	Ladies' Maid 2
Army Pensioner 1	Farm Bailiff 1	Land Agent 2
Asst. Schoolteacher 2	Farm labourer 27	Laundress/ Maid 6
Baker 1	Farmer 16	Hawker 1
Baker/ Farmer 2	Farm Assistant 7	Lunatic 1
Blacksmith 4	Farrier 2	Maid 2
Bootmaker 3	Footman 3	Mason 3
Bricklayer 6	Gamekeeper 4	Midwife/ Nurse 2
Builder 2	Gardener 13	Schoolmaster 1
Butler 1	Gen. Labourer 23	Needlewoman 1
Carpenter 1	General servant 3	Painter/ Decorator 1
Carter 11	Grocer 5	Parlourmaid 1
Cattle/ horse dealer 3	Grocer Postmaster 1	Pauper 1
Charwoman 1	Groom 4	Physician 1
Clerk in Holy Orders 1	Hall boy 1	Plasterer 6
Coachman 6	Head Carpenter 1	Police officer/Constable 3
Cook 2	House Steward 1	Postboy/ clerk 2
Dairy work 7	Housekeeper 3	Rector 1
Decorator 1	Innkeeper 2	Road contractor 1
Domestic servant 6	Kitchenmaid 3	Shopkeeper 1
Dressmaker 9	Labourer 5	Saddle/Harness maker 3

Sawyer 2	Shirt Seamstress 1	Tutor 1
Schoolmistress/ Maid 2	Shoeing smith 1	Valet 2
Scullerymaid 1	Stableman 3	Washerwoman 2
Servant 6	Stillroom Maid 1	Woodman 1
Shepherd 4	Thatcher 1	Working Bailiff 1

East Knoyle has always been a unit composed of separate parts. As well as the three formal 'tithings' of Knoyle, Milton and Upton, other settlements had, and have, a distinct identity. With four farms, a baker's shop, a general stores, a carpenter, a thatcher, a lace maker, a weather prophet and an undertaker, Holloway people at the turn of the 19th and 20th centuries took special pride in their self-sufficiency. Many of these can be traced from census returns and from the Holloway sketch map in the scrapbook.

No. 1 on the map, down Holloway Lane, was where Mr Shepherd lived ('The Old Pheasantry'). He supplemented his income as a gamekeeper at Clouds by selling a pair of rabbits at 9d. (4p) to favoured customers. He also collected herbs from the woods and fields. These he made into a potent-looking black ointment which he sold in small tins for all sorts of ailments. Many of his clients used to say that they never needed to see the doctor.

At Nos. 2 and 3 (Sunnyside and Bluebell Cottage) were Mr and Mrs Davy Fletcher, Mr and Mrs Ben Grey and their families.

No. 4 (Paddock Wood) was the home of Mr James Snook; carpenter, undertaker and weather prophet. He had two daughters: Mary and Jetty, nicknamed Martha and Mary on account, it is said, of their characters (!).

'Old Holloway', with its houses and their occupants around the turn of the 19th to 20th Century.

At No. 5 (Allens) lived Josaiah Moxham, who was a sidesman at St. Mary's. He was well known for his instruction of 'Pass the sasser', when he handed the collection plate to members of the congregation at the start of each row.

No. 6 (Copse View) was the home of Alfred Street and his wife Julie, together with their three children at the time of the 1881 Census. He was a gardener.

Charles Street, who was a carter, lived at 'Capua'. Next to him, at Holloway Cottage, were James Neil (or Neale), originally from Fonthill Gifford, Ellen and their family. On one day in May, the chimney at their farm caught fire at around midday, just as the men were returning to their cottages round about for their dinner. Everyone turned to, but in the strong wind the thatch was soon alight. The buildings were gutted despite the efforts of the Clouds Fire Brigade who were soon on the scene. They could do little as the only source of water for their hose was the well beside each cottage.

Mr Edward Scammell and his wife Lucy lived at Old Orchard, and carried on a laundry business. One relation, Mrs Betsy Scammell, lived to be 101.

Opposite Old Orchard lies Glebe cottage, then two properties belonging to the Rectory. Mike Nisbeck, the Milfords' coachman who lived next to the Rectory, is shown on the sketch map driving the open Landau in his (blue) uniform with white facings and cockaded hat. The other part was where Eli Tuck the gardener lived.

Thomas Snook at No. 11, who had been a bootmaker, was followed there by Mr and Mrs Frank Smith.

Opposite Paddock Wood lived Charles Lampard, (grandfather of Mrs Elliott at Bell Cottage) in the cottage now known as 'Little Thatch' – which had once, apparently, been a weaver's cottage. He was a thatcher who also made bee skeps from straw. When he died, Mrs Maidment, originally from Buckingham, moved in. She was a brilliant needlewoman, employed as a seamstress at the Rectory. She also made exquisite lace and was often to be seen at her doorway on fine days, with her pillow and bobbins.

Mr and Mrs Woodley lived in what is now, confusingly, known as 'The Old Rectory'. When Canon Cross moved out of the original Rectory in the 1930s, he made alterations at the late-17th-century Holloway Farm before occupying it and renaming it 'The Rectory'. The former Rectory was sold by the Church to the Fison family, who renamed it 'Knoyle Place'. When Knoyle had to share its Rector with Hindon, Chicklade and Pertwood in the 1977 parish reorganisation, the old Holloway Farm was sold, though a small plot alongside remains church property. This now – on the strength of 40 years' existence as the priest's house – became 'The Old Rectory'(!).

The last house in Victorian Holloway, just below Cleeve and opposite Little Lye, was the bakery where William Burb(r)idge and his family lived (Orchard House). His bread, dough and cakes did a brisk trade.

Soldiering

The presence of Knoyle men as Troopers in the Hindon Militia Troop at the time of the 'Battle of Pyt House' in 1830 has already been mentioned. No detail has come to light of Knoyle men (other than Percy Wyndham) being involved in the Crimean War. According to Canon Milford, writing in the parish magazine, there was a long list of men with Knoyle connections to be prayed for during the Boer War. One of his daughters helped to answer an appeal from the 2nd Battalion the Dorset Regiment for comforts to be sent out. Particularly wanted were men's handkerchiefs and bootlaces. Happily, with one exception, all the Knoyle men from what the Rector called 'a long list', without giving details, returned safely. Lance Corporal W. Sanger, whose grandmother lived in the village, died of enteric fever in Pretoria, the South African capital. At this period, before the importance of applying strict health and hygiene precautions had been fully recognised, it was common for over six times as many men to die from infected wounds or fever as were actually killed in battle.

One regular army soldier who came to live in Knoyle was Sergeant Fowler of the Dorsetshire Regiment. After service in the United Kingdom, the East Indies and Aden, he retired at the age of 42 in about 1902 and came to live in Underhill with his wife and their daughter Kathleen Lucy. Their home was what is now known as 'The Cocked Hat'. He died in 1910. Knoyle men served in the Wiltshire Rifle Volunteers before World War I.

Sergeant Fowler and his wife, on his retirement from the Dorsetshire Regiment. They settled in Underhill, in what is now known as 'The Cocked Hat'.

Manoeuvres were held on Salisbury Plain, usually as in 1872, with a march past at the end. There was a big muster at Summerleaze in 1910, when Percy Wyndham and his family in their open landau joined many other residents to view the proceedings. Between the Wars, Knoyle men trained and went to camp for the war which, at one time, few believed could ever happen.

Quite a number of former and serving soldiers sailors and airmen have had homes in and around the village, including two brothers who took part in the Gulf War.

Sport and Relaxation

Mrs Elliott, writing about the village as it was before World War I, recorded that 'a Public house was not a necessity, as the farmers brewed their own beer: 'large' for the family and 'small' for the farm labourers.' Farmhouse cider was also made regularly. The last local farmhouse cider maker lived just over the boundary in West Knoyle parish, and had a good number of regular customers, especially at weekends. The writer found the product very acceptable, but it was best drunk quite soon after purchase, as it became a bit rough later.

Necessity or not, there was an alehouse in Milton, and three others in the parish. The *Black Horse*, in The Street, was the headquarters of the Friendly Society. The *Seymour Arms*, a bit further south on the line of the Roman road , dates back three centuries or more. Until the middle of the 19th century, it was called the *Benett Arms*, after the owners of Pyt House. It changed its name, to become more 'politically correct', when Henry and Alfred Seymour were building up their Knoyle estate and becoming the leading family in the parish. The *Fox and Hounds*, up at the Green retains its thatch and has a bowling alley which doubles as a function room.

Cricket was played on a pitch at New Close, between the Broadmead and Summerleaze ponds, very close to the footpath. It was from that Summerleaze Fish Pond that ice used to be transported to the Knoyle House Ice House. The Milford family and their staff provided members of the team around the end of the 19th century, and the village eleven played in local leagues between the Wars. The pitch has gone and there is no team now.

The football pitch used to be at Gasson, beside the A350 opposite Park Farm. There are photos of trophy-winning teams in the first half of the 20th century, and the club survived with occasional hiccups until it closed down in 1981. Part of the ground was swallowed up by the bypass. The team played in local leagues. The needle matches would be against Hindon, when, according to one source, 'there would be one battle on the pitch and another off it afterwards' – a bit of an exaggeration, perhaps!

The bull pits in the woods above Summerleaze were the venue for bull baiting, until it was banned by Act of Parliament in 1835. Being in such a remote spot between Knoyle and Hindon, it is possible that watchers may have been set to keep a lookout for some while after this.

Badger baiting is an illegal activity thought to have long died out in this part of the country. It is understood that the recent discovery of snares and stopped-up earths in the parish may be an indication of animals being trapped to be transported up north.

Industry

*B*rickmaking and tiles. The brickyard was on the West Knoyle road leading to Lugmarsh Farm. Bricks were first made there in the 1790s. The clay was dug out and stacked in heaps to weather it. Trolleys then transported it to the pugmill, which was a steam-powered device for grinding and mixing clay. From there it was run into brick moulds. The sand used in brick manufacture was taken from the sandpits at the junction of Holloway, Underhill and Constitution Hill – the last name pre-sumably dating from 1689 'The Glorious Revolution' when James II was displaced by William and Mary. Before World War Two, the Parish Council at one time charged one shilling (5p) for a cart-load of sand. Payment was made through the Post Office, from where one collected the key to unlock the bar across the gateway. The Council also used the pit to dispose of tins and bottles from their monthly refuse collection.

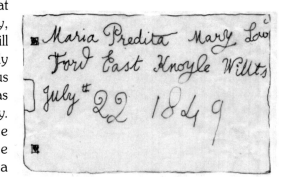

Tilemaking. This is a half-size drawing (here further reduced) of a tile found at Orchard Cottage (now Orchard House) in Holloway. It was apparently made by an Italian worker and measured 10 ¾inches by 6 ¾ by ½ an inch. Sand came from the sandpits at Constitution Hill, stone from Cleeve Hill and lime from the lime kilns on the Hindon road. Firing took place at what was formerly known as Brickyard Farm.

Charcoal Burning. This was carried out in Park Copse at least until the start of World War Two. Inside a cone covered with wet clay slabs to exclude air, kindling wood started the process by igniting the lumpwood to be turned into charcoal. Smoke and waste gases escaped through a funnel outlet at the point of the cone. The burning was a skilled process, and entailed watching the cone for about a week. If a strong wind blew, this could be enough to make the smouldering fire break out, in which case the whole batch would be lost. Wet clay was always kept handy day and night to plug any leaks in the slabs.

Lime Burning. Lime is a valuable rural product, useful for conditioning the soil, whitening walls and mortaring stones. The village kiln was on the Hindon road towards Sheephouse, where there has been landfill in recent years. It was working until 1931. There was stabling for two horses and a hut for a watchman to be on duty at night. The Village Scrapbook describes the process used: 'Holes were drilled, then fuses of gunpowder inserted, three at a time, to blow out the chalk. This was then put in the two kilns to burn, with layers of anthracite [better for the purpose than coal] and chalk alternately.' Once the kiln had burnt out and cooled down, the contents were raked out of the bottom hole of the kiln. The lime could then be slaked with water.

Road and Building Stone Quarrying. Stone for roads and drives came from Haddon Hill. Before the days of steamrollers, this roadstone would be just thrown down on to the surface, to be crushed by the traffic and hobnailed boots. Building stone, a distinctive green sandstone, was quarried at Cleeve, very close to Chapel Farm. Some would be sawn, but less important surfaces could be trued up with an adze. The stone for the Primitive Methodist Chapel next to the *Fox and Hounds* came from this source. Some of it was carried by Mrs Hetty Fletcher and other women in their aprons.

The Chase

In the early mediaeval days, before Selwood Forest was 'disafforested' in 1330, the deer would have been hunted on the land to the west of the Shaftesbury road. Similarly, they would have been shot with the bow in the Bishop's park, Park Copse. Its extent was bigger then – right out to the deer leap ditch behind the houses on The Street – before the Park Mead fields were carved out for development, a process known as 'assarting'.

Foxhunting

There has been foxhunting in the vicinity of Knoyle at least since 1655. William Willoughby and his friends plotted 'the rising at Sarum' from his home in West Knoyle in the course of the Civil War under cover of a week's hunting. His relative Christopher took an active part in East Knoyle parish affairs after the Restoration of Charles II.

The Arundell family of Wardour Castle ran a pack of hounds in south-east Wiltshire for almost a century from 1690. In the west, a pack owned by the Horlocks, father and son, hunted in the 1820s and 1830s. Alfred Seymour hosted a meet at Knoyle House in 1849. However, he turned up so late that the day's hunting had almost been abandoned by the time that he arrived.

Local hunt members were prepared to ride to a meet, or in the later Victorian period to send their horses by train; for the majority of venues could be ten or more miles away. For them, the formation of the West Wilts Hunt in 1868 was very welcome. Three years later, the separate South and West Wilts Hunts were united to form the South & West Wilts Hunt under the West Wilts Hunt Master, Colonel John Everett.

Some meets assembled near to the coverts which would be drawn first. Others, known as 'lawn meets', were held at the home of a prominent supporter. In Knoyle, Alfred Seymour at Knoyle House and later on Percy

The South & West Wilts Hunt meets at Knoyle House before WWI.

Wyndham at Clouds House would most likely provide a champagne breakfast for the field and followers before the hunt set off at around midday.

Hounds are counted in 'couples'. At the time of writing there are 28 couples housed in the kennels built by Lord Stalbridge at Motcombe in the early 20th century. The expense of maintaining the pack and paying hunt staff has always been a problem – and caused a number of masters (who often bore much of the cost) to resign.

Subscriptions from hunt members, the Supporters' Club, the Car Followers and the profit from Point to Point racing, are supplemented by riding and social events of many kinds. The Hunt Pony club and appearances of the pack at agricultural shows such as the local Gillingham & Shaftesbury one help to keep the Hunt in the public eye.

Up until the Second World War, foxhunting was a generally accepted part of rural life, providing much more than sport for farmers and the gentry. Many country people took part and others were employed directly or indirectly using their specialised skills and crafts. As well as the dedicated and knowledgeable hunt staff, this included: farriers, grooms, boot and saddle makers, tailors, hedgers, carpenters, woodland managers and conservators, gate and jump makers (to combat the evils of barbed wire) – and many more. Nowadays, farm hands are almost an endangered species, with relatively few people earning their livings from the land.

Across the nation, attitudes have changed and become more polarised.

Peace and War

When King Edward VII died in 1910, the clouds of war were beginning to form, though few realised what 'Kaiser Bill' (The Emperor Wilhelm II) was up to.

Life at Knoyle went on much as before, with occasional local excitements. One such was witnessed as a boy by Alfred ('Alfie') Tanswell. He was watching estate workers cutting furze to repair the shelter on Percy Wyndham's golf course during the winter of 1910/11. The offcuts were burning on a bonfire set dangerously close to the old windmill when some of the sparks set the wood alight. Fortunately, the Clouds Fire Brigade was quickly on hand to douse the flames. The mill had not worked for 25 years. The sails and superstructure were decayed but the tower was still a village landmark. The fire did a limited amount of further damage but was a foretaste of things to come.

The Knoyle windmill in 1873, from a watercolour by Jane Bouverie. The mill ceased to grind corn 13 years later.

George V and Queen Mary's Coronation day was set for 22nd June 1911. A village committee was formed and stewards recruited to repeat the pattern of Edward VII's Coronation ten years before. The programme they decided upon was to be followed in outline through royal, victory and millennium celebrations for the rest of the century.

*The windmill on King George V's Coronation Day, June the 22nd 1911. The
proclamation over the door says 'GOD SAVE THE KING!'*

At 2.30 p.m. the Knoyle Band marched to church from the school. The
bells were rung for a short service. Afterwards separate teas were provided for
adults and children, while the Band played in the Rectory garden. The Band
then led a procession of flag-waving children up Windmill Hill for a sports
programme, with the Band playing again from time to time. Refreshments
(non-alcoholic) were dispensed by the Ladies' Tea Committee.

At dusk a magnificent bonfire was lit on the forward slope, from where
a further dozen could be seen. Then there were fireworks, let off from the
windmill platform. A misdirected rocket set the remaining woodwork ablaze,
but this time there was no reprieve. The cap was totally destroyed.

The programme ended with the Band playing the National Anthem at 11.30 p.m. During the next week, the Rector presented Coronation mugs (without handles) to the 200 schoolchildren.

The windmill was not allowed to fall apart. George Wyndham rebuilt the top as a lookout over the Blackmore Vale. The machinery was removed.

When war broke out on 4th August 1914 the Territorial Army was mobilised, the Wiltshire Rifle Volunteers having Knoyle men amongst them. Many young men answered Lord Kitchener's call and became part of 100,000 volunteers. Eighteen men did not return, five of them from just two families: the Jolliffes and the Wyndhams. Their names were set on the War Memorial erected on the corner of The Square in 1919, as well on the memorial in the church, all too soon to be added to. Together with the dead from Semley and Sedgehill, the roll of the fallen from the two World Wars is read out in St. Mary's church on Remembrance Sunday.

The disastrous blaze on Coronation night. Note the ladder up to the cap on left. The photograph was taken by A Cole, said to have been a member of Clouds estate staff.

Growing food became a top priority, while at the same time government agents scoured the country to seize suitable horses for the Army. Mr Jefford successfully hid his two magnificent beasts, which were saved to 'plough and mow, to reap and sow'

A meet of the South & West Wilts Hunt by the windmill after the fire; showing the sails still attached to the spindle. Before he died in 1913, George Wyndham had had the mill top sealed and the present wooden superstructure built as a lookout over the Blackmore Vale.

*Ernie Mallett (far side) with a Thornycroft lorry in France during WWI. Note the
solid tyres.*

*Farming in wartime. The Hull family at Sheephouse Farm in 1916. Mr Michael and
Mr Edwin Hull's grandfather (also Edwin) is standing at left. Next are:
Mr Gray, Sammy Matthews, Ted Coombes and other members of the Hull family.
Mr Charles Jefford is holding the horses which he hid from the military contractors
seeking to requisition suitable animals for the battlefront in 1914.*

throughout the war. Women were organised to work on the land, initially under male supervision (of course!). In World War Two the Wiltshire County War Agricultural Executive Committee took No. 21 The Street as a hostel for some 20 Women's Land Army girls, whose numbers were swelled by their boyfriends from London at weekends. Later on the hostel was closed and accommodation provided in the bothy at Knoyle House. Most of the girls did gang work such as harvesting and threshing.

A notable evacuee who came down to Wiltshire for a year in 1916 was Lucien Pissarro, the eldest son of the French Impressionist painter Camille. Brought up in France in extreme poverty, he had become London-based by 1914, obtaining British citizenship two years later. After three months in Sedgehill, he came to Knoyle in October. He lodged first at 'The Enterprise' (now 'Tower House'), then at Moorlands, The Green. During this period he

A view of Milton, painted by Lucien Pissarro during his year-long stay in Knoyle.
From a private collection.

painted over 30 local pictures. Though now widely dispersed, most have been traced and are instantly recognisable today. In true Impressionist style, some detail was transposed or omitted altogether if the artist felt that this would enhance the overall effect.

The twenty years between the wars brought lean times for many people in the countryside; from estate owners crippled by death duties to farmers struggling to make a living during the agricultural depression. World War One had widened people's horizons, with new means of communication: transport, radio and telephone creating new opportunities.

The first public motor transport for the village was provided by Mr Rawlings of Hindon. He ran regular outings to places of interest such as Bournemouth and the Cheddar Gorge. At first the vehicles had solid tyres,

An outing to Bournemouth beach in about 1924. Left to right: Mrs Evelyn Tanswell, Evelyn Francis (Mrs Roberts),Harold & Phyllis Garrett and their mother. Mrs Tanswell's mother, on right, is still having to walk with the aid of a stick. She had been struck by a motorcycle when coming out from a WI meeting at the Village Hall.

which must have made them pretty uncomfortable to ride in for any distance. The first East Knoyle bus service was operated by Messrs Macbeth and King, with a bus called 'Sally'. Later Mr Bartlett took over. The first private car that appeared in the village was owned by Mr Edward Gordon, who lived in 'The Enterprise' at Church Rails.

Village organisations flourished. These included the British Legion and the Scout Troop led by Mrs Neville, the Rector's wife, with adult support from others, such as Mr Frank Barnes, who had been appointed headmaster in 1910 and was to continue in office until his retirement in 1948. There was also the Women's Institute (W.I.), the Mothers' Union, the Choral Society, and the Girl Guides.

Lady Pembroke was an active President of the W.I. for many years and supported many of the other organisations. She was loyally assisted by her son the Honourable Colonel Herbert and later by her grand-daughter Miss Guendolen Wilkinson.

When war came again in 1939, many of the young men once more took up arms, but everyone was involved. Rationing, blackout, Air Raid

An early motor car outside Tuck's stores. This machine, registration number Y 2573 was first registered on June the 8th, 1914 to John Willis of Porlock. A 20hp 4-seater, originally black but later painted brown, it was intended for use as a 'public conveyance'. In 1917 it was sold to the Porlock Weir, Porlock & Minehead Motor Service Co. Ltd. In 1920, it passed though Yandle & Sons of Ilminster to Tom Parris of the George Inn Chardstock, near Chard.

Members of the Boy Scout Troop founded by the schoolmaster Mr Frank Barnes take tea at Clouds, attended by three of the household staff.

Wardens, Firewatchers all became a necessary part of daily life. The Wiltshire County War Agricultural Executive Committee sought to tell farmers how to do their job, but also provided equipment resources on which to draw. With invasion across the English Channel a very real possibility in the summer of 1940, the Local Defence Volunteers - soon to be renamed the Home Guard - came into being.

No. 3 Wiltshire Battalion was formed on 16th May under the command of Col Sir George Herbert T.D., with its Headquarters at Knoyle House. It consisted of six companies; with 'E' Company covering: Chilmark, Tisbury, Hindon and East Knoyle with Sedgehill. The Company Commander was Lt Col C.T. Marshall Smith. The Knoyle Platoon, which had some Sedgehill men in it, was commanded by Knoyle farmer Mr Reginald Jesse.

At first the arms were pitifully inadequate – six Short Lee Enfield rifles per company, shotguns, pickaxes, pikes and bludgeons. When the Battalion was stood down this had grown to: Standard .303 inch rifles, light and medium machine guns, Sub machine guns (the Sten gun, which was easy to set off accidentally) Spigot mortars and six two-pounder Anti tank guns.

In July 1940, when attack appeared imminent, each village and town mounted a patrol of one NCO and six men during the hours of darkness. The 'Dad's Army' television series has given so many hours of enjoyment that it is easy to forget that many of the Home Guard men were veterans of what used to be called 'The Great War', with lots of battle experience, even if a quarter of a century before.

The Knoyle platoon operated from the bothy at Knoyle House, though the platoon photograph was taken outside the Seymour Arms (!).

Colonel Herbert died at Bath on 20th January 1942, 'to the great grief of all who knew him'. His Second-in-command Major G.M. Atkinson was promoted and appointed to succeed him. One year later the Battalion HQ moved to Warminster.

A parade was held at Warminster on 16th May 1943 to mark the third anniversary of the Battalion's formation. Music was provided by the Pipe Band of the Fife and Forfar Yeomanry stationed in the town, and 1,750 all ranks out of a total strength of 2,278 marched past Brigadier Grigson Ellis OBE late of the Grenadier Guards, who took the salute.

The stand down parade took place 18 months later, on 3rd December 1944, by which time all danger of invasion had clearly passed. The bugles and drums of the 3rd Wiltshire Battalion, Army Cadet Force led the contingent this time, which was inspected by the Lord Lieutenant, Colonel the Duke of Somerset. The numbers on parade were rather lower, 1,107 all ranks out of a possible 2,138.

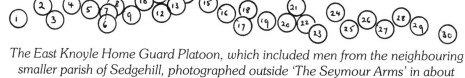

The East Knoyle Home Guard Platoon, which included men from the neighbouring smaller parish of Sedgehill, photographed outside 'The Seymour Arms' in about 1942. Those identified are:

1. 2/Lt Cyril Hyde
2.
3.
4. Mr Harris (of Waterdale)
5. Mr Tom Harding
6. Sgt Charles Jefford
7.
8. Mr Bert Nisbeck (Seymour Arms)
9.
10.
11.
12. Lt Reginald Jesse (Pl Comd)
13.Mr Bert Chubb
14.Mr Sidney Penny
15.Col (HG Major)Marshall-Smith
16.
17.

18. Mr Harold Tucker
19.
20. Mr Brockway
21. Mr Ernie Burton (Glebe Cott. Holloway)
22. Mr Frank Jesse (cousin to Mr WJ Jesse)
23. Mr Cochrane (kept the shop at The Green)
24.
25. Sgt Rocket
26. Mr Sidney Gray
27. Sgt Goodship
28. 2/Lt Dick Bartlett
29. Mr Bill Clements (Garage owner)
30. Mr Lew Lever (Keeper, Bramble Cott.)

There are two recorded royal visits to Knoyle during World War Two, both with a kind of military connection, the first literally so. King George V's widow Queen Mary was due to lunch at Knoyle House one day early in the war, before the Honorary Salvage Officer of Mere & Tisbury Rural District

Council had won his battle against Knoyle House by taking away the railings for scrap (for which they were virtually useless). A tank sped round the corner of the Square, supposedly steered by braking the tracks on one or the other side of the vehicle. The driver lost control and mangled a section of the ironwork. Lady Pembroke and her staff wasted no time in removing the debris, so that all was under control when Her Majesty arrived.

The second occasion went more according to plan. King George VI and Queen Elizabeth came to Summerleaze to inspect the troops drawn up on the common. Afterwards they returned by Millbrook Lane to the A350.

When peace came after nearly six long years, the cost in Knoyle lives was mercifully lower, but a dozen men were still lost.

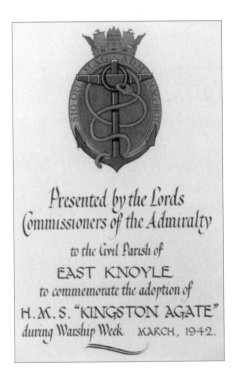

Presented by the Lords Commissioners of the Admiralty

to the Civil Parish of

EAST KNOYLE

to commemorate the adoption of

H.M.S. "KINGSTON AGATE"

during Warship Week   MARCH, 1942.

HMS 'Kingston Agate', whose adoption was shared with the neighbouring parish of Sedgehill, had a lively time in WW2. The 464 ton vessel was built in Hull in 1937 for the Kingston Steam Trawling Co., but requisitioned by the Royal Navy in 1939. On April the 14th 1941, together with her sister ship HMS 'Kingston Amber', she shot down a German Heinkel 111 bomber aircraft with machine gun fire. Four months later, she played a leading role in capturing a German submarine (U470), unable to dive after being bombed by a Hudson aircraft of RAF Coastal Command. She survived the war, was returned to her owners in 1946 and sold to Belgium for scrap in 1964.

Ghosts?

It is, perhaps, only to be expected that an ancient village such as East Knoyle would have its share of experiences not readily attributable to natural causes.

In the middle of the last century, a newly retired couple were looking for a property to buy in the village. A 'period' cottage with good views looked promising, so they arranged to meet the house agent at the site. To their surprise, he refused to accompany them inside. When pressed, for the prospective buyers were not of the kind to stand any nonsense, the man admitted that he had felt a 'presence' in the house and a misty shape had appeared to come through a wall upstairs. They did not buy the house, though not on account of the 'presence'. Subsequent owners have noticed nothing unusual.

A former churchwarden, who was very down to earth with a wide experience of life, used to mow the greater part of the old churchyard, including the slope behind the church building. Although the experience was not an alarming one, he regularly felt that someone was standing behind him, watching while he worked in that area. A similar sense of being watched has been felt by a man working in an old property elsewhere in the village.

When Ann Harding was gatekeeper at the Turnpike, there was a farrier's shop at a cottage nearby, to attend to any horse that had cast a shoe. A recent owner used to tell of hearing hoofbeats in her yard.

Some years ago, two children were staying with their grandmother in the southern part of the village. The lean-to scullery had recently been converted into a bathroom next to the kitchen. One morning as the children came downstairs they both looked into the bathroom, seemed surprised by what they saw and went to find Granny. Their question was: 'Who is that old lady in the funny long dress in the bathroom?' The cottage had been occupied a good many years before by an elderly couple.

There is a house in the Northern part of the village where an unexplainable knocking could be heard on some evenings. There was nothing sinister about this – and the owners referred to the source as 'George'.

At a property in another area, a series of circumstances occurred of sufficient substance to call for investigation:

- Noises and footsteps were heard at half past nine at night;
- There was a 'cold spot';
- The noises and footsteps, as well as lights unaccountably being turned on, increased when one of the owners enlarged an upstairs bedroom which jutted out over the neighbours' wall;
- The dog used to bristle for no apparent reason.
- A family member became aware of a man in tweeds on the stairs – whom the investigator identified as 'a teacher';
- An oldish thickset lady in 19th-century dress was seen. The investigator named her 'Emily'.

Mr John Tanswell, first headmaster of the village school in Church Road, lived in a cottage close by. His wife's name was 'Emma' not 'Emily; although there was an Emily Tanswell in the parish. After the investigation, things quietened down somewhat.

The strangest account of a happening came from a lady who formerly lived in the village. What follows is taken from a tape-recorded interview with her conducted by the author.

There's a lot of history in that house. There was a trapdoor. They pulled it up with a rope ladder, to stay out of the way of robbers. We took it down when we knocked it (two cottages) into one. Then we boarded the trapdoor in.

Under the floor, first it was bricks, then it was sand, then it was rushes, all strewn. It's over 400 years old. At one place the spade went right in deep. The man that was digging thought it was where the hearth had been, leading up to a hole in the thatched roof, before the days of chimneys.

Well, it started then . . . the thing used to come up the ladder at night. It would go through the bed over the place we filled in, straight through the wall where the door used to be, until we changed it for a bathroom.

In the end, a workmate of a member of the family put a wooden cross under the bed. Later I could feel the thing coming – it was all cold. It came up to the cross at midnight, went down and never came again.

In the same house, a later occupant reckoned to have seen a ghost, who was not unfriendly. 'He's perfectly all right', he said, 'but he's murdered his wife.'

Seven Notable Knoylians

Sidney Jukes

Mr Charles Jukes was landlord of the Fox & Hounds in the early years of the 20th century. His son, Sidney, was an outstanding pupil at the village school, who then went on to further his education at night school. He was also a Server at St. Mary's church.

When World War One came, he volunteered for active service. He qualified as a pilot with the fledgling air force, then known as the Royal Flying Corps. As a bomber pilot, Lieutenant Jukes Royal Air Force flew operational sorties in France in 1918, as well as becoming a pilot instructor.

Lt Sidney Jukes with colleagues in front of one of their bomber aircraft during World War One. The officer on his left has clearly been seconded from the Argyll and Sutherland Highlanders!

Tragically, he was killed in a flying accident in dense fog in Cheshire on 27th November 1918, just after the Armistice. The beautiful processional cross in the church was given in his memory by the Matron and staff of St. George's Hostel, Plumstead,

At his funeral in the village, the RAF provided a military band and a firing party who discharged three volleys over the grave. Many of his colleagues joined the mourners – a special tribute to a remarkable man.

Guendolen Wilkinson

Guendolen Wilkinson first came to the village when visiting her grandmother Beatrix, Dowager Countess of Pembroke and Montgomery, at Knoyle House. Later on, she was to live with her for much of the year, taking a significant part in running the domestic affairs of the estate. She took a leading role in the 1st East Knoyle Guide Company, taking over its leadership

Guide Captain (later Commissioner) Miss Guendolen Wilkinson with three of the Guides: Alice Francis (Mrs Beard), Florence Durrant and Winifred Fletcher.

in 1925 when Miss Selina Doggrell was forced to resign through ill health. Up until World War Two she spent a lot of time in London, doing charitable work – and became involved with the Girls Guides there also. Every year she had a camp set up on the Knoyle House side of New Close, visited by 40 to 50 girls over a three-week period.

She was very tall, with a commanding presence, and took an active part in many village activities. She trained as a nurse at Salisbury General Infirmary during World War Two. In 1943, together with Miss Ada Blake, who became the Matron, she set up and ran the 'Beatrix Nursery' named after Lady Pembroke. This was a baby home of the 'Waifs and Strays', later renamed the Church of England Children's Society. At first it was located in Knoyle House, before transferring to Clouds. Clouds was a recognised training school for nursery nurses, some of whose graduates still live in the area. The Society became concerned about the expense of maintaining the property; so that on the 1st June 1964, when Matron Miss Blake and Sister Miss Wilkinson retired, it closed its doors. The two ladies bought 'Cleeve' and retired there, purchasing Orchard Cottage for staff. Later, they moved to Orchard Cottage (which had been the old bakery in Holloway) themselves. When they did so, they named their new home 'Guenada', but it is now known as 'Orchard House'.

Guendolen was the daughter of Sir Neville Wilkinson, Ulster King of Arms, whose lasting achievement outside his work was to create 'Titania's Palace' for his daughter. He made and furnished this fairy fantasy in miniature down to the tiniest detail. The present Queen and Princess Margaret spent several happy hours there on a visit as young children. It is now possible for the general public to share their enjoyment, but the firm of Lego eventually purchased it so they have to go to the company's headquarters in Copenhagen to do so.

Until she died in 1987, Guendolen maintained a kindly but firm interest in the village and its people, especially the children. The skittles boards, which are still hired out for use at fêtes today, were bequeathed by her to the village, but woe betide anyone who let them get wet or be otherwise neglected!

One of Guendolen and Ada's pleasures in retirement, after Guendolen gave up driving, was to be taken by Miss Margot Sully into Salisbury for a shopping expedition each Thursday. The highlight was holding court in Marks & Spencer's while the manager and staff attended to their weekly order.

Alice Francis (Mrs Nelson Beard)

A lice Francis was a Guide in the 1st East Knoyle Guide Company and Brownie Pack just after World War One.

In 1935 Alice and Miss Jeffcot took over responsibility for the Brownie pack and ran it for a year. They then handed over in turn to Mrs Winifred Bartlett (née Stevens and now Hyde), who had been a Guide in the same Company.

Alice worked in the Post Office then run by Mr Henry Burton at Black Horse for 12 years. One day, Miss Wilkinson came in to ask her if she would consider becoming Lady Pembroke's Ladies' Maid across the road at Knoyle House.

After a couple of days' careful thought she agreed and took up residence – with her private room immediately above Lady Pembroke's looking west across The Square towards the church.

Her working day began at a quarter to eight. Precisely at this time she would be handed a tray on the landing with Lady Pembroke's breakfast.

After breakfast, when Lady Pembroke was dressed, Alice would spend the morning working with her. At first this would often be needlework; but later on she kept the accounts, under her mistress's watchful eye. Lady Pembroke was a kindly person, popular and much respected in the village. By the time that Alice came to work for her she was no longer young, but continued to take a personal interest in every member of the community, especially the staff and children at the school. As Founder President of the East Knoyle Women's Institute and President of the East Knoyle Branch of the West Wilts Conservative Association, she was in a good position to know what was going on and to provide a helping hand where she thought it necessary.

Each day Alice would have some time to herself. As a senior member of the domestic staff, there was a strict understanding that she was responsible to Lady Pembroke, and that she was not to be imposed upon. On Sundays, the family would attend to Lady Pembroke's needs, not Alice.

During World War Two Alice had to take her turn at 'firewatching' patrolling round Knoyle, although she never in fact had a fire to report. Alice eventually married PC Nelson Beard and went to live in the Police House.

Constable Beard was one of the last of the old-style 'village bobbies'. Local crime was at a low level. Young and old found him firm but fair; able and willing to take corrective measures when necessary before anything serious happened – sometimes in ways that would not pass muster today. After he retired, he and Alice went to live in her family cottage on Hindon Lane. The property is now known as 'Deepwater Cottage' in reference to finance rather than to topography.

PC Beard was honoured by being chosen as one of the recipients of the Queen's Maundy money, when Salisbury Cathedral was the venue for her to make her annual distribution.

Although increasingly troubled with arthritis in her later years, she never lost her zest for life, her sense of humour or her keen recollection of past times in the village.

Mr Frederick (Freddie) Francis

This account is taken from his obituary in the newspaper in May 1962. As it gives a lively picture, and ties in with recollections passed on by members of his family, it is reproduced in full.

Mr Freddie Francis of Restcroft, East Knoyle , . . . aged 74, will be remembered as one of the old country boys of the farming world, having lived all his life in the village of East Knoyle. He could plough, mow, reap and sow.

Mr Francis had lived in three different cottages in Milton, where he was formerly employed by the Hon. Percy Wyndham, on the Clouds Estate, and was for many years a cornet player of the old East Knoyle Village Band, during the period of the rousing Knoyle Club days. In later years, after the break up of the Wyndham estate, he was employed by the late Mr Thomas Hyde, at Valley Farm, Milton.

He then moved into the cottages of mud' (actually 'cob', lumps of clay mixed with straw) 'at the lower end of Milton, opposite the blacksmith's shop and the Milton sheep dip. The cottages were built [by William Mallett] entirely of mud, instead of sand and cement. It was from here that Mr Francis would fetch Mr Thomas Hyde's herd of cows early in the mornings from the meadows, around Sutton Bottom, and drive them along the road the entire length of Milton to Valley Farm for early morning milking.

For the rest of the day he would most probably go to and fro, through Milton with the horse and cart doing various kinds of work. During the haymaking period Mr Francis used two heavy horses to pull the grass cutter around the field and when it came to the actual haymaking he used the hand-operated horse drawn hay rake, raking the hay into neat lines across the field ready to be swept into the hayrick. At corn harvesting time he cut the corn with the horse-drawn binder when three horses were needed to pull this machine around the field and made and shaped the cornricks using the battering board.

From Mr Hyde's orchard at Milton, Mr Francis would take cartloads of sacked cider apples to Mr Green's farm, on the turnpike, where there was a cider press, and later through East Knoyle, brought back barrels of cider. He was also a very good ploughman and was often seen at Milton Hollow with two horses tethered to a single-furrow plough.

When Valley Farm at Milton was sold Mr T. Hyde went to live with his son Mr C. Hyde at Milton Farm, and Mr Francis was employed there, having moved into a cottage much nearer the farm. Being somewhat musical, he was often seen in the garden or in the cottage sat in a chair playing his melodeon or push button

Mr Freddie Francis and his wife. On at least one occasion he played his accordion for skating on Broadmead pond, coming back with a capful of coins.

accordion, and was most popular in the village inns. He once was invited to play to a group of ice skaters one winter's evening on Broadmead pond, which had frozen over. [On that occasion his cap was well filled with coppers from the appreciative skaters] Mr Francis was also very popular with his accordion music at the Over Sixties Club in East Knoyle Village Hall, to which he belonged after retiring from farm work. He did odd gardening jobs around the village after moving to a cottage on the Turnpike.

In 1960 he and his wife . . . celebrated their golden wedding. He will be sadly missed in the country life of the village . . . , this likeable, gentle farm worker who had given so much of his life to agriculture.'

Mr Ernest Littlecott

E rnest Littlecott was born and grew up in Hampshire, coming to Knoyle at the age of 18 in 1902. At that time his father was shepherd in charge of Mr Percy Wyndham's large flock on the Clouds estate. He assisted his father, with one short break in 1916, until the Clouds estate was broken up after World War One. He then went as shepherd to Mr Bradshaw of Milton Farm, and to Mr Reginald Jesse who succeeded him. Finally, he worked for Reginald's son, Mr John Jesse, until his retirement after 50 years service as a shepherd. As a young man, he played the clarinet in Miss Marion 'Mai' Milford's small orchestra. With Walter on the 'cello, Frank on violin, and Edwin on cornet, it was almost a Littlecott ensemble.

He also learnt to play brass instruments, studying under Bandmaster Carter of the 1st Wilts Volunteer Rifle Corps and later in the 4th Battalion the Wiltshire Regiment. He played in both the Hindon and East Knoyle Bands, rising to become the Knoyle Bandmaster. He also enjoyed choral singing, being a member both of St. Mary's church choir and of the Village Choral Society – which competed successfully at Wiltshire County Music Festivals.

He was a member of the Parochial Church Council for some years and a sidesman. He was a member of the bellringing band when the bells were taken out in 1933 and removed to the Whitechapel bell foundry for turning, retuning and partially refitting. One year later they were back in the tower, but hung in a different and more logical order, which caused a few problems at first.

Sheep dipping at Milton. Left to right: Mr Les Goodship, Mr Penny, Mr Ernie Littlecott.

The East Knoyle Band after WW1. Mr E Littlecott (cornet) centre seated, Mr Jolliffe at back in cap (drum), at 5 o'clock from him Mr Alfie Sturgess, 3rd from right Mr George Snook, extreme right Mr Fred Francis (cornet).

He was a regular member of the cricket team for many years.

He belonged to the National Union of Agricultural Workers and was a member of the Independent Order of Rechabites (a benefit society for total abstainers).

At his funeral, taken by the Rector, the bells were rung muffled in a mourning tribute.

Mr Frank Barnes

Mr Barnes was appointed headmaster on 1st April 1910 at the young age of 26. Three years later he married Mrs Barnes and they came to live in Church Cottage, where they remained.

One of his first initiatives outside the school was to found the Scout Troop, of which he was first scoutmaster. He was immensely proud of his pupils, of whom he demanded and got a high standard of academic work. He was able to work smoothly with the school managers and with three Rectors. Canon Milford retired soon after he arrived, but both Mr Neville and his wife were very supportive. This was carried on by his successor, Canon Cross.

During his 55 years in the village, there was hardly an organisation or event in which Mr Barnes did not have some official status or interest. In the church he was Secretary of the Parochial Church Council, a member of the choir and a lay reader for 22 years. He was a Parish Councillor, being elected chairman for a period of 20 years.

Mr Frank Barnes (centre rear) with the Scout Troop which he founded.

He was active on the Village Hall Committee and in the Horticultural Club, also taking on the post of Secretary of the Village Charities. He was a member of the Shaftesbury Freemasons' Lodge. On a personal level, he was ready to offer help and advice when asked. He served as a Special Constable in both World Wars.

Perhaps his most lasting contribution to the community was his work in researching its history. He was noted for his talks on the village's past, particularly its links with Sir Christopher Wren. He gave great assistance to the Women's Institute in their epic compilation of the three original village scrapbooks.

Mrs Barnes, though diminutive in size, was a strong character, who also played a significant part in the life of the village. With Lady Pembroke, she was a founder member of the W.I., its first Secretary,

Presentation to Mr Barnes on his retirement as Headmaster after 38 years.

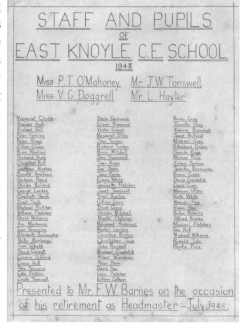

later Vice President and finally President. For 43 years she was Secretary and Enrolling Member of the Mothers' Union.

Mr and Mrs Barnes celebrated their Golden Wedding Anniversary in 1963. Mr Barnes died three years later. When the house was emptied, a few valuables were sold but his papers on parish history were simply burnt. Some of that material was irreplaceable.

Mr Alfred ('Alfie') Tanswell

Finally, to a man whom the writer felt privileged to have as a friend and neighbour. Alfie was born and bred in the parish, being christened at the church in Pertwood, now no longer part of Knoyle.

Educated at the village school, he went to work as part of the outside staff at Knoyle House. He was a stalwart member of the Football eleven in the 1920s, with a reputation as a robust and skilful goalkeeper.

During World War Two, he served at RAF Tempsford, servicing the Lysander aircraft used by the Special Operations Executive for inserting and extracting Allied agents from France.

The East Knoyle Football XI 1933/34: Winners of the Shaston Thresher Challenge Cup and the Dinton Tournament Cup. Back row: Penny (Groundsman), Col the Hon. George Herbert (President), W Fletcher, J Few, C Robson (Capt), A Tanswell; Centre row: H Hull, F Scammell (Vice Capt), K Doggrell (Treasurer); Front row: H Sheen, J Street, A Sheen, J Rawlings, W Scane.

When the war ended, he became a lengthsman for the County Council. It was always possible to tell when one was entering 'Tanswell territory' as the whole stretch would be immaculate.

His garden at Haddon Houses was a showpiece: A riot of colour in the summer, where no weed dared to take root, or got short shrift if it did. When, as a widower, he and his neighbour Miss Emmy Fletcher both moved to the new bungalows in Church Rails he left his garden in first class order. The next tenant allowed it to become a jungle. He set to work again, and soon the new plot was being raised towards the standard of the old.

He believed in the worth of the work done by the British (now Royal British) Legion and was Escort to the Standard for many years. Even when his eyesight began to fail, he supported the East Knoyle Branch as long as he was physically able to do so.

The People and the Place

There has been little change in the population of the village at about 850 or so over the last hundred years; although its makeup has markedly altered.

The large landowning families of Seymour and Wyndham – employing numerous staff for indoor and outside work – have gone.

Not only has the original rectory (now 'Knoyle Place') become a private residence, but its replacement also ('The Old Rectory' in Holloway). The Rector himself now lives at the Semley rectory, with responsibility for three parishes. Under the Salisbury diocese plan for the next stage of reorganisation, he or his successor is set to take on a further two parishes: making five in all with six churches.

Old village family names are still to be found, though not necessarily closely related (if at all) to those noted in the old parish records. Their number is dwindling. Some have been around for hundreds of years.

First recorded in:	Name:
1549	Fletcher (John)
1582	Burbage (Matthew)
1585	Burton (Richard)
1610	Snook (Leonard)
1635	Bartlett (Bridgett)
1658	Lampard (Edward)
1664	Scammell (Charity)
1754	Maidment (James)
1799	Jolliffe (William)

There was a single 'Hull' (Isabell: *sic*)) recorded in 1566, though there is then a gap until the 19th century. The first Parish Council was elected in 1894. In 1896, Mr Edwin Hull stood as a candidate and was successful in the following year (Parish Councils were then elected annually). The family proudly claim to have had a member on the Council ever since that time, giving over a century of service.

There are more military and ex-service families in the village than there were a century ago. Many people have sought properties in the parish for their retirement. When an owner-occupied 'period' cottage in what house agents call 'this sought-after village' becomes vacant, it will usually be sold at a high price. After modernisation, the property will either become a cherished home, or be sold on at a profit.

Some residents have been able to purchase their council houses under the 'Right to Buy' legislation. When the late Colonel Stephen Scammell was building up his post-World War Two new Clouds estate, he took steps to provide a number of village residents with cottages to rent; but otherwise the stock of affordable housing available either to rent or buy is low.

A growth area is in 'Second Homes'; where the owner can relax and escape from the stress of business or city life. Many 'Incomers' have contributed greatly to the wellbeing of the community over the years; playing as full a part in its life as they can. Without such commitment, the village is the poorer.

Pluses and Minuses

A hundred years ago, the village had three places of worship. The Primitive Methodist chapel was founded in 1843 at a time when the movement was becoming strong in Mere, Motcombe and the surrounding areas. The existing Ebenezer Chapel building, just above the *Fox & Hounds* at The Green, dates from 1857. In its early years, there were congregations of 90 and 79 at the afternoon and evening services. The social side was not neglected, with the refreshment at their tea parties being of a particularly high standard. The chapel closed and was sold some years after the end of World War Two. It is now a private house.

In 1848 Canon Milford's immediate predecessor, the Reverend Morgell, was appointed Rector. At that time Mr Herbert had been the Baptist minister with responsibility for Knoyle. He was actually a 'paedobaptist', meaning that unlike the mainstream Baptist Church, he favoured baptising infants rather than adults.

According to the 'Centenary Celebrations of the East Knoyle Congregational Church' Mr Morgell 'Represented to Mrs Penny (who owned the building) that he was sympathetic (to the Baptists) and induced her to sell the chapel to him. Having got possession of it he immediately turned the people out, asserting that he would soon put down dissent in his parish.

'Thus driven from their beloved sanctuary, they were obliged to worship in a house belonging to one of the members. About three years later the Lord interposed for them by disposing the heart of our dear friend Mr Jukes (of Mere) to build the present beautiful and commodious chapel.' It opened in 1854.

The Reverend Milford was less extreme, but relations were icily correct rather than cordial. Happily, by 1954, 'If the characteristic of church life in 1854 was strife, that of 1954 is unity.' Excellent relations between St. Mary's and the Congregational Church (which became part of the United Reformed Church (URC)) continued until the end of Pastor Edith Young's ministry. She was a retired schoolteacher from the North of England: golden-hearted, firm minded and with a special interest in the village school (of which she was a governor) and its children. Sadly when she retired for a second time, she was not replaced.

The last URC service in Knoyle was on 26th October 1986. The congregation included not only the URC members but also many friends from St. Mary's. Mrs Albert Sully, the organist for 70 years, played one of the hymns in a moving final gathering. Mrs Clifford Burton, whose family had run the Post Office for 107 years, was elected a member of St. Mary's Parochial Church Council with acclamation at its next meeting.

Knoyle House has gone. In its last days before being sold and demolished for its lead, wood and fireplaces it served as an Old People's home. Medical supervision was in the hands of a Matron; but the establishment was run by an enigmatic individual, who wished to be known as the Reverend Russell and used to preach from time to time at the Chapel. According to recollections from village sources, it appears that he held a service in St. Mary's Church while the Rector was away on holiday. The Reverend Palmer returned unexpectedly early, to find the service in progress. Since he had given no permission, the proceedings were abruptly halted.

Through the timely action of Mr Feldgate Catt and a vigorous campaign to collect village contributions, 'Knoyle House Ground' was bought in 1975 as a permanent open space for recreation in the village.

Clouds House has survived. After the Duke of Westminster (Bend Or)'s short tenancy, Adriaan Mosselman, his wife Nancy and their family lived there in some style until 1932. Dick Wyndham then sold outlying properties, furniture, fittings and books. The staff were not generously treated. The estate was put on the market, remaining unsold until 1936, when it was bought by property speculators in London – who had visions of lots of 'des res' development.

In the event, the Houghton Brown family acquired the house and most of the surroundings. They decided to reduce the house to a manageable size,

Mr Michael Hull with US Sergeant Eugene Tuxcotte, formerly of the 3rd (Spearhead) US Armored Division on their visit to mark the 50th anniversary of D-Day In 1994.

(above) The commemorative plaque presented to the village 50 years later by veterans of the 3rd(Spearhead) US Armored division to mark their time in Knoyle while preparing for the D-day landings in Normandy in 1944.

```
                                        P A R T   I.

Part Songs:

        Orpheus with his Lute      ..       ..      German
        The Flowering Manger       ..       ..      Buck
      . The Frog      ..      ..             ..      Newton

              Mrs. K. Turner, Mrs. G. Forward
              Mrs. C. Hyde, Miss K. Pletcher
              Mrs. Frazer, Mrs. H A. Fulford
                 Miss A. Long  Accompanist


Sonata No. 2 for Violin and Piano
    in one movement        ..      ..       ..      Delius

              Betty Richardson:   Violin
              Joyce Honner:       Piano


An Eriskay Love Lilt  ..       ..        ..      Anon
If Thou Art Near      ..       .         ..      Bach
To Daisies      ..       ..       ..        ..      Quilter

        Patience Cross:        Soprano
        Chaplain Joe O'Rillion
        (U.S. Army).          Accompanist

                   INTERVAL
```

(above right) Part of the programme for a concert during 'Salute the Soldier Week', held in the Village Hall on the 22nd of May 1944. At least two of the artistes remain in the village and will recall being joined by Chaplain Joe O'Rillion of the US Army, sparing time to act as accompanist in the midst of preparations for the Normandy invasion. This actually took place just over a fortnight later.

but had particular difficulty with the tower. In the end the Royal Engineers took on the task of blowing it up, succeeding at the third attempt.

When World War Two came, the family moved out to 'Cleeve', a house on the other side of the hill. Clouds became a secretarial college, with the Army requisitioning part of the basement and putting up Nissen huts in the grounds.

Units of the 3rd (United States) Spearhead Division arrived in preparation for the D-Day landings in Normandy in 1944. They brightened up the social life of the village, and the soldiers made friends with some of the youngsters. When former members of the Division returned with their wives 50 years later, contacts were renewed. A bronze plaque on the wall of the Village Hall records their visit, presented by the veterans; while they received a framed copy of the newly completed illustrated village map.

When the Army and the secretarial college moved out, the Beatrix Nursery moved in. When it closed in 1964, Colonel Stephen Scammell was keen to prevent the destruction and possible unsuitable development of a property which had happy memories for many village people – who had only recently seen the destruction of Knoyle House in the village centre.

Purchase was arranged, repairs undertaken, and the house let as a school 'for maladjusted boys'. Relations with the village were sometimes a bit bumpy. However, several boys joined the church choir and the school had links with the Football Club, using the pitch on Gasson by special arrangement.

By 1983, the school had closed. Clouds now entered into the latest phase of its existence. It has become a drug and alcohol dependency treatment centre, run successfully by the Life Anew Trust.

When Knoyle ceased to be an all-age school, with over 150 pupils, numbers naturally declined. The events leading to the last ten children departing and the doors being closed in July 1984 have left scars which have yet to heal over completely. They will not be set out here.

It is clear that without a school actually located in the village, an important focus for the children is lost, and the community thus weakened. Fortunately, the combined school at Hindon is 'St. Mary's and St. John's School' retaining a Knoyle connection in its title. The Parish Council, St. Mary's Church, Knoyle-based School Governors, parents and individuals continue to give the thriving school their support.

The *Black Horse Inn* in the Street, once headquarters to the old benefit Club, is now a private house, including the part which provided the Post Office until it moved to its present location. The *Seymour Arms* and the *Fox and Hounds* continue to slake the thirst and banish the pangs of hunger of village people and visitors.

The Fox & Hounds Darts Team sets off for Southsea 1954/55. Left to right: Ted Allen, Doris Hall, Winifred Bartlett (now Hyde)- owner of the coach, Doug Bagg, Tom Hall (Landlord), Garth Gray, Den Hall, Bill Campbell.

The fortunes of clubs and societies go up and down everywhere. East Knoyle still has quite a number, though modern lifestyles and work patterns make it often difficult to find people with the time and the commitment to run them. Those which have stayed the course over the years include:

• The East Knoyle, Semley and Sedgehill Branch of the Royal British Legion, with its Women's Section, maintains a lively presence; ensuring that 'We will remember' the fallen and those who need help now. With support from all over the village, large sums are raised for the Poppy Appeal, and there is an active social programme.

• Scottish Dancers and The Physically Handicapped Club meet in the Village Hall each week – which the Hall committee works hard to keep as one of the best in the county. Mrs Isabel Seymour, who built it in 1908, would be proud of them.

• The East Knoyle, Semley and Sedgehill Branch of the Conservative Association is the only formal party political presence in the village. The Westbury constituency has returned a Conservative MP for many years. The Parish Council is apolitical.

Recent casualties include the Women's Institute, revived in the '90s, but now in 'suspended animation'. Wren's Group of the World Wide Fund for Nature (WWF), sustained for over a quarter of a century by a nucleus of dedicated workers, was enormously successful in raising funds. It has now ceased to operate.

The Youth Club is in abeyance, after over 37 years of providing a valuable facility for the young people.

On the positive side, when the Knoyle Branch of the Mothers' Union (founded by one of Canon Milford's daughters) fell on hard times, a decision was taken to transform itself into an open club, the St. Mary's Guild. This has an active membership. The masonic Lodge of Innocence and Morality, which met in Hindon under its Master, James Ames (the village surgeon), from the end of the 18th century until 1832, has been revived and meets in the Village Hall. The church bells have been rung for services since before 1553 and the present day Band continues to do so as an active part of the Mere Branch of the Salisbury Diocesan Guild of Ringers.

Other organisations set up in the last few years are:

• The Garden Club, which holds lectures and discussions and arranges visits to places of horticultural interest. It donates some of the funds it raises to the Village Hall.

• The Mothers' and Toddlers' Group.

• The Church Youth Group, which chose to be known as 'The Cool Christians'; meeting once a month, and from time to time making an imaginative contribution to Family Services.

The most significant event for the village in the last 50 years has been the opening of the bypass.

Ever since 1935, there had been talk of the need for one. A route mapped out by the County Council would have taken the new road westwards towards the church, into Park fields and eventually back on to the A350 south of the Police House. During World War Two, as mentioned earlier, a tank knocked down the railings at Knoyle House just as Queen Mary was due to come to lunch. The passage of tracked vehicles down The Street immediately before D-Day was also an earth-shaking experience. Even so, in 1979 the County Surveyor went on record as saying 'There is no prospect of the East Knoyle bypass being considered in the County Council programmes for the next five years'.

During that time: A child was tragically killed, walls were being almost routinely knocked about and pedestrians were having to become ever more agile in dodging the increasingly heavy traffic using the improved port facilities

The problem speaks for itself. This sort of jam was a regular occurrence at two choke points in The Street and Hindon Road.

at Poole. In two particular places, as the Director of Highways reported: 'Heavy goods vehicles cannot pass or do so with extreme care.'

At last, in 1989, the County was moved to act. A consultation document was produced. Our County Councillor, Mr Robert Catton, wrote an article in the village newsletter, summarising the options on the basis that the County Council had agreed that construction of the East Knoyle bypass should begin in 1992. A well-presented exhibition in the Village Hall in March with Council officials on hand attracted much attention and there was a good take-up on an accompanying questionnaire. The Parish Council, while aware that some businesses stood to lose their passing trade, dismissed the 'Red Route', which would have merely shaken foundations at the back of the houses instead of the front. In their preferred solution, they supported the 'Yellow Route' somewhat further to the East, with some modifications to improve safety. At the same time a number of objectors sought and obtained a measure of support for a more easterly route which would arch round up the hill towards Hindon at about the area of the old limekilns.

The controversy was heightened when residents of The Street managed to get the County Council Highways Committee to come down in December 1990 to see for themselves. The traffic was held up for a short while as a protest was staged calling for the bypass to be started on the Yellow Route without further delay.

The County Council now accepted the need for some urgency, but funding remained a problem. After a number of false dawns, Transport Secretary John MacGregor announced on 15th December 1993 that Government money would be made available in the financial Year 1994/95.

Even now, the saga continued. A Public Inquiry to consider objections was held in the Village Hall in July 1994. Once again, there was a demonstration. This time notices were put up saying 'Bypass now' and yellow balloons carried the same message. A good-humoured balloon-carrying group of men, women and children, with their babies and dogs, awaited the Inspector at the Village Hall gate.

The demonstration with posters and yellow balloons on the day of the public inquiry into the bypass route in July 1994. Unfortunately the media were not present to record it. Mr Michael Head resolved this by having the scene recreated the next morning. Here he is marshalling the demonstrators for the repeat performance.

The Inspector conducted the proceedings with scrupulous fairness. Only at the end did he allow himself to remark 'Yellow Balloons will always have a special meaning for me!'

The Inspector's recommendation to proceed was accepted, most of the objections having been resolved. The final stages in the sequence of consultation produced some further concerns, but they were addressed.

The bypass route under construction, looking from North to South. The site office is visible at the bottom of the picture.

Mrs Joan Main (Chairman of Wiltshire County Council) cuts the tape to open the bypass, with the help of the Chairman of Highways, The Chairman of Salisbury District Council and Knoyle's County Councillor Robert Catton (at right) – March the 6th 1996.

A procession of village people, determined to be the first to travel the bypass, even in the sleet. Note the miniature fire engine (not needed) at the rear.

The County Council Direct Works Organisation won the contract in open competition. The first turf was cut by County Councillor Robert Catton and Parish Council Chairman Mrs Mary Streets at a ceremony on 12th May 1995.

Work proceeded apace. On Friday 6th March 1996, on time and within budget, the bypass was opened by the Chairman of Wiltshire County Council cutting the tape. A shower of sleet failed to dampen the spirits of those assembled to watch the ceremony or the procession of village people up the road, determined to be the first to use it officially, and accompanied by a miniature fire engine!

John Chandler leaps for joy down the centre white line of the former through route, watched by Alison Borthwick and Simon Hunt – an impossible manoeuvre before March the 6th.

People marvelled at their ability to walk unimpeded down The Street. Parents now felt confident in allowing their children to go unescorted on to the Knoyle House Ground play area, free from traffic fumes and snorting lorries. Householders no longer feared for their walls. There was a well-attended street party at the *Seymour Arms*.

Not everyone stood to gain. Due partly to increased speeds, sound reflections off a screening wall and the type of surfacing used on the road, the noise level has increased noticeably in some parts of the village. Businesses

18.8 Two residents from opposite sides of The Street celebrate at the open air party held at The Seymour Arms.

like the Post Office shop, the garage and the *Seymour Arms* felt vulnerable to loss of passing trade, which the placing of some signs on the bypass would not be sufficient to prevent. As the Parish Council regularly reminds people: 'Use them or lose them.'

Conclusion

East Knoyle has been a recognisable community where people have lived and worked for over a thousand years. Its original roots go much deeper, before written records began.

No one can predict the future with any accuracy; but so long as its people care enough, it will always be a very special place.

Appendix 1

The two versions of Domesday Book

for Chenvil (East Knoyle)

Exon Domesday: [A draft, compiled for part of the south west of England.]
Chenvil. The King has 17 ½ hides in demesnes, the Abbot of Glastonbury 5 hides, the Abbess of Wilton 4 hides and one virgate, Walter Giffard 4 hides, Gilbert Maminot 3 ½ hides and ½ virgate, Godric, huntsman, 1 virgate and for 51 hides are paid to the King £15-16-0 (£15.80). But of this were not paid 74/- from Knoyle Regis - land of Earl William-, at any of the usual terms, but for it the four collectors of tax retained 12 pence. Saulf, however, retained the tax of 1 hide, 1 virgate which he holds of Gozelin de Riveire, to wit 7/6.

Domesday, final Version: The King holds Chenvil, Aileva held it in the time of King Edward and it paid geld for 30 hides. There are 15 ploughlands. In demesne are 17 hides and a half, and there are 5 ploughs and 10 slaves. There are 16 villeins, 18 bordars and 18 coscets, with 10 ploughs. There are 15 ac* of meadow, and the pasture is one league long and as much wide. Of this land Gilbert has one hide. There are three bordars. It is worth 7 shillings and 6 pence. It was worth £28: It is now worth £30.

*By the late Stephen Scammell's reckoning:
'15 ac' i.e. 'acti quadrati' = about 5 acres;
The pasture was about 609 acres;
The wood was about 304 acres.

Appendix 2

Selected Field and Farm Names

(A more complete list, with locations, is being compiled for the Village Archive)

Celtic	
Pertwood	'perta' = a copse
'Clouds'	once thought to be connected with 'clwyd' is derived from its owner in 1581, John Cloud.
Saxon	
Bratch(es)	land recently taken into cultivation.
Culverhayes	'culver' = woodpigeon, 'hayes' see below.
Hanging	'haenga' = a wooded hill e.g. Holden's Hanging, Warminster Hanging.
Hay(es)	'haeg' = a fenced-in piece of land e.g. Bramble, Broad, Great, Jupp's, Holm, Vetch.
Leigh(Lye)	'leah' = a clearing e.g. Upper Leigh, Lower Leigh, Little Lye.

Moot Field   'moot' = meeting place.
Plashet   'plaescet' = a shallow pool.
Slades   'slaed' = a short valley.
Summerleaze   'laes' = pasture.

Norman / Old English
Barn's Hill   a corruption of 'Baldwin'. Oswald Baldwin, of Flemish stock, came over with the
                        Normans. He held two hides in Upton.
Steeple Close   in this case, 'steeple', from Old English = a steep wood.

Allotments from the breakup of the Common Field system, subsequent landholders, glebe (Church land)
Allotment   allotment: From enclosure awards e.g. Park, 1st and 2nd, Shaftesbury;
Ground   ground: As above e.g. Slade's, Home, Thorn's, Gould's, Cuff's, Perman's, Bennetts,
                        Marchant's, Carey's, Huntley's;
Field   former common field (see above), but may also refer to an allotment or just be an
                        identification for convenience;
Coleman's Farm   named after a 16th-century owner;
Friar's Hayes Farm named after a 17th-century owner;
Glebe   often with no other name, but can be further identified e.g. 'Parson's Field';
Close, Rails   an enclosure: Long Close, New Close, Brown's Close, Ox Close, Wood Close, Doctor's
                        Close, Church Rails;
Great Ganns   derivation unknown. Traces of mediaeval ridge and furrow cultivation visible within
                        living memory.
King's Bushes   named after a 14th-century owner.
Tenantry Down   land farmed by the tenants. Named to distinguish it from the Lord of the Manor's
                        land (known as 'demesne') farmed by him.

Unusual Names
Bath
Bunches or
Barber's Mead   by Wise Lane, mediaeval oxen ploughland; 'Bunches' could be 'benches', in allusion
                        to the ploughing ridges;
Colonel's (!)
Gasson
Heaven   in Clouds Park;
Kite's Nest
Picket/Peaked Field with sharp corners;
Puxey
Skiddy Axe   in the Haddon stonecutting area;
The Drot
Throdmill   by the windmill.

Notes

The Beginnings

1. SKIPWITH, G.H. *Folklore Gatherings from the Western Counties, Folklore 5* 1894 pp339-40.
2. *Victoria County History(Wiltshire)* (VCH) Vol. I, p67.
3. *Wiltshire Archaeological Magazine* (WAM) Vol. L p102.
4. Possibly Ronald Garrett, or a member of his family at 'The Lookout'.
5. BARNES, I Lecture to Shaftesbury & District Archaeological Group *The Archaeology of Salisbury Plain* c1998.
6. *VCH* Vol. XI, p83.
7. AC Archaeology excavation for Wilts CC 1995, as reported to Shaftesbury & District Archaeological Group.
8. BORTHWICK, A *East Knoyle News Letter* September 1995.
9. TIMPERLEY, H.W. & BRILL, E. *Ancient Trackways of Wessex* Phoenix House, London 1965.
10. CUNLIFFE, B *The Ancient Celts* Penguin, London 1997. p189.
11. JAMES, S *Exploring the World of the Celts* Thames & Hudson, London 1993.
12. Iron Age Museum, Andover, Hants.

The Romans

1. GRINSELL, L.V. *The Archaeology of Wessex* Methuen, London, 1958.
2. FIELD, N.H. *Dorset and the Second Legion* Dorset Books, Tiverton, 1992.
3. BERRY,B *A Lost Roman Road* Allen & Unwin, London 1963.
4. DE LA BEDOYERE, G *Roman Villas and the Countryside* Batsford/English Heritage, London 1993.
5. HEALD, H (Ed) *Chronicle of Britain & Ireland* Chronicle Communications, Farnborough 1992.
6. *The Common Ground Book of Orchards* Common Ground, quoted by B Juniper in The Times 13 Jan 2001.

The Coming of the Saxons

1. For an evaluation of these and other sources, see JOHNSON, S *Later Roman Britain* Paladin, London 1982.
2. SCAMMELL, S.E. *East Knoyle The History of a Wessex Village* David A.H. Grayling, Crosby Ravensworth 1996.
3. Ibid.
4. FAULKNER, N *British Archaeology* quoted by N. Hammond in The Times 14 Dec 2000.
5. OMAN, C *A History of England* Studio Edition, London 1993 p263.
6. FOOT, S *By Water & the Spirit - Pastoral Care Before the Parish* , BLAIR, J & SHARPE, R(Ed) Leicester University 1992.
7. PARKER, D & CHANDLER, J *Wiltshire Churches* Alan Sutton, Stroud, 1993 p78. In discussing the phenomenon of church groups in Anglo-Saxon England, John Blair notes the recurrence of churches dedicated to St Mary, linking this to early Christian practice: *Pastoral Care Before the Parish* cf. Note 6 above. Michael Franklin, quoted, by S Foot, defined a 'minster' as 'a church originally, or vestigially, with pastoral responsibilities for an area larger than a single village: FRANKLIN, M.J. *The Identification of Minsters in the Midlands* Anglo-Norman Studies, 1984.
8. In discussion with the late Alison Borthwick a tentative attribution to the 9th to 11th Centuries was reached. The lack of readily identifiable detail means that the cross could date from the 12th Century, or even later.
9. YORKE, B *The Anglo-Saxons* Sutton Publishing, Stroud 1999 p100.
10. FOWLER,P.J. & CLUTTON-BROCK, J *The Archaeology of Anglo-Saxon England* WILSON, D.M.(Ed) Methuen, London 1976.
11. *Encyclopaedia Britannica*, Vol. VII, p987.
12. MacDONALD, J *Monarchs, Murder, Mystery & Mayhem* Wilts County Council 2000.
13. CHURCHILL, W.S. *History of the English Speaking Peoples* Vol 1, Cassell, London 1956.

The Normans

1. PARMENT, R *The Castle of Robert the Devil* A Vallee, Rouen p3.
2. *Encyclopaedia Britannica* Vol. IV p807.
3. MESSE, Y *Petites Histoires de Temps Passe en Pays Cormeillais* Editions Bertout, Luneray c1995.
4. *Victoria County History, Wiltshire*: Vol. II, p67.
5. HEALD, H (Ed): *Chronicle of Britain and Ireland* Chronicle Publications, Farnborough 1992 p191.
6. SCAMMELL, S.E. *Roman Saxon & Norman Units of Measurement in Domesday Book* David A.H. Grayling, Crosby Ravensworth 1995.
7. BRYANT, A. *The Story of England* Collins, London 1954.

The Village Community Takes Shape

1. *Close Rolls of Henry III 1263*, researched by SULLY, W.H.C. East Knoyle.
2. This account comes from a combination of sources, especially the *Victoria County History, Wiltshire.(VCH)*
3. HUDSON, W.H. *The Illustrated Shepherd's Life* Savitri Books, London 1987 pp18-19.
4. HOLT, R *The Mills of Medieval England* Basil Blackwell, Oxford ISBN 0-631-15692-5.
5. *VCH Vol XI.*
6. JOHNSON, C.R.I. *History Verses* Aymestrey School Worcs c1940.
7. SMETHURST, A.F. *The Pictorial History of Salisbury Cathedral* Pitkin, London c1960.
8. HEALD, H (Ed) *Chronicle of Britain & Ireland* Chronicle Publications, Farnborough 1992.

The Black Death and its Aftermath

1. For a thorough investigation of bubonic plague and an analysis of its effects see: ZIEGLER, P *The Black Death* Folio Society, London 1997.
2. Presented in the Channel 4 programme 'Secrets of the Dead - The Riddle of the Plague Survivors' in March 2002.
3. Thanks to the efforts of Col. AW Gough-Allen.
4. SCAMMELL, S.E *East Knoyle The History of a Wessex Village* David A.H. Grayling, Crosby Ravensworth 1996.
5. See VCH and BUSH, R *Somerset, The Complete Guide* Dovecote Press, Stanbridge 1994.
6. Principal sources of information on the Goldsborough family were: BENETT-STANFORD J.M.F *Families of East Knoyle -* *The Goldesboroughs of Upper Leigh* 1945; the *Victoria County History of Wiltshire Vol XI; The East Knoyle W.I. Scrapbooks* and the *East Knoyle Parish Registers.*

Henry VIII, The Seymour Family and the Reformation

1. MEE, A *Wiltshire, Cradle of our Civilisation* Hodder & Stoughton London 1939.
2. ibid.
3. There are two references for this, both presumably quoting village tradition.
a. Mr B STRATTON, a local historian and longtime Knoyle resident who did much of the research for the village W.I. Scrapbooks.
b. Notes of a lecture to the W.I. by Mr F BARNES, also a local historian and well respected as village headmaster for 38 years.
4. The Sale Catalogue quotes Dr WAAGEN *Treasures of Art in Great Britain II* p241 as attributing 'this version possibly to Holbein himself on the grounds of its long connection with the Seymour family'. It was exhibited at the National Portrait Exhibition, South Kensington Museum in 1866, and was photographed at Knoyle House in 1882. The catalogue also states that the portrait belongs to a group of which the archetype was a wall-painting executed by Holbein for the Privy Chamber in Whitehall Palace in 1537. The original was lost in the palace fire of 1698, but a smaller copy exists at Hampton Court.
5. ASTON, M *Monasteries* Batsford, London 1993.

The Wren Connexion, Civil War and Monarchy Restored

References consulted in the preparation of this chapter:
BEARD, G *The Work of Christopher Wren* Bartholomew, Edinburgh 1982.
BENETT-STANFORD, J *Notes for a History of East Knoyle 1939* (East Knoyle Archive).
BRIGGS *Wren the Incomparable.*
British Museum MSS of the Falstone Committee 1647.
British Museum; Addl MSS 22,084
CHAMBERS, J *Christopher Wren* Sutton Publishing, Stroud 1998.
COLT HOARE, R *Hundred of Mere,* 1822.
CUNNINGTON, B.H (1934) Transcription of East Knoyle Court Baron 1658.
East Knoyle Archive (STRATTON,B and others).
FAIRFAX, J.E *When Baptism was banned by*

Parliamentary Ordinance The Clifford Association Newsletter, Vol I No.12 1989.

JERRIM, E.R *Notes for a Book on the History of Hindon.*

MacLACHLAN, T *The Civil War in Wiltshire* Rowan Books, Landford 1997.

New Sarum Quarter Sessions Records 1651: Chilmark Rate for East Knoyle poor.

Oral traditions collected by the late Mrs Olive Steedman, Valley Farm, East Knoyle.

PUGH, R.B *Old Wardour Castle* HMSO, 1968.

Register of Sequestrations for Wilts British Museum MSS 164-9.

SCAMMELL, S *East Knoyle: The History of a Wessex Village* David A.H. Grayling, Crosby Ravensworth 1996.

STRATTON, B *East Knoyle Vestry Meetings & Village Notes c1950* (East Knoyle Village Archive)

Victoria County History (Wilts) Vol XI.

WAYLEN, J *Christopher Wren of East Knoyle D.D.* Wilts Archaeological Magazine.

WEBB, G *Wren* Great Lives Series.

WHINNEY, M *Wren* Thames & Hudson 1971 .

WREN, Dr C *Family Notes c 1650.*

WREN, S *Parentalia*

Changing Times: The Eighteenth Century

References:

East Knoyle Village Archive.

Charity Commission Scheme 134(S)/75 27 March 1975. Ref: 1678-5-11-73X(2).

MICKLEBURGH, R Transcripts of Charity donors' Wills.

MORLAND, T *Two Wessex Roadways* Wiltshire Industrial Archaeology No.5, 1974.

Crime and Punishment

References:

COBLEY, J *The Crimes of the First Fleet Convicts* Angus & Robertson, 1970.

East Knoyle Church Guard Book 1890.

Gaol Calendar, Easter 1785, Wiltshire & Swindon Record Office. (WRO).

JOHNSTON, Dr D of King's Worthy, Hampshire; whose assistance in the preparation of this account of James Wigmore's death is gratefully acknowledged.

Major Ross' Returns (Commandant of Royal Marines, First Fleet) p236.

PROTHERO, L *Cross: His Mark* Lorraine Prothero, 7 Morshead St, North Ryde, 2113, Australia 1987.

Richards' Returns (First Fleet Contractor) p256.

Salisbury & Winchester Journal: 14 & 28 Feb, 7 14 & 21 Mar 1785.

WRO A1/125/46C.

Hard Times

1. BURNETT,J *Our Changing Fare* McKenzie & Rudkin London, 1966; quoted by HOBSBAWM, E.J. & RUDE, G in *Captain Swing* Lawrence & Wishart 1969.

2. Mere Historical Society: *The History of Mere* Blackmore Press, Gillingham 1958.

3. New Encyclopaedia Britannica, 15th Edition.

4. BRYANT, A *The Age of Elegance* Collins, London 1950.

5. *Captain Swing* vs.

6. MUIR, R *The Countryside Encyclopaedia* Macmillan, London 1988.

7. VCH Vol V.

8. *Captain Swing* vs, p363.

9. STRATTON, B Notes in East Knoyle Archive.

10. CHAMBERS, J *Wiltshire Machine Breakers Volume I.* Jill Chambers, 54 Chagry Close, Letchworth 1993. Jill Chambers' readable and meticulously researched account includes reference to eyewitness accounts. The original documents (@ WRO 413/23) make fascinating reading at the Wiltshire & Swindon Record Office, but are reproduced in the book.

11. WRO 413/23.

12. ibid.

13. CHANDLER, J *East Knoyle News Letter* Jan 1996.

14. CHAMBERS, J vs. (PRO WO13/4044: Muster Rolls of the Wiltshire Yeomanry)

15. HUDSON, W.H. *The Illustrated Shepherd's Life* Savitri Books 1987, p153.

16. Notes by BEGG, J.L. pupil to BROWNING, J - Estate Agent to Percy WYNDHAM.

Georgian and Victorian Seymours at Knoyle House

References:

BURKE, Sir B *Burke's Peerage, Baronetage and Knightage* London, 1933,1949.

Illustrated London News 12 April 1856.

Victoria County History Vol XI 1980.

Women's Institute Scrapbooks for East Knoyle.

WRO: The Seymour Estate Game Book.

The Wyndhams

The information on which this chapter is based has been collated from many sources including present and former residents of Knoyle. These include the following publications:

DAKERS, C *Clouds, The Biography of a Country House* Yale University Press, New Haven & London 1993. This has been an invaluable guide to further local research in the village.

ASQUITH, C *Haply I may Remember* James Barrie, 1950.

ABDY, J & GERE, C *The Souls* Sidgwick & Jackson, London 1984.

BLOW, S *Broken Blood.*

BLUNT, W *Country Life* 19 November 1904

OLIVIER, E *Four Victorian Ladies of Wiltshire* Faber & Faber, London 1945.

RIDLER, G *Bend'Or* Robin Clark Ltd, London 1985.

MacKAIL, J.W. & WYNDHAM Guy *Life & Letters of George Wyndham.* Devon County Library.

MILFORD, T.R. *Two Brothers, a Milford Memoir* Oxfam, 1986.

TENNANT, Pamela *Village Notes* Heinemann, London 1900.

WYNDHAM, G *The Ballad of Mr. Rook (With illustrations by The Hon. Mrs. Percy Wyndham)* Smith, Elder & Co., London 1901.

WYNDHAM, J *Wyndhams & Children First.*

YOUNG, E *The History of East Knoyle School* 1984.

East Knoyle Parish Magazine 1909-1911.

Burke's Peerage, Baronetage and Knghtage 1933.

Other sources gratefully acknowledged are:

The East Knoyle W.I. Scrapbooks.

Mrs Winifred HYDE of Milton.

Mrs Mary HALL of Warminster.

The Milfords

1. The prime source of information on family detail was material kindly made available by Mrs Ann Ridler, daughter of Violet Bradby (nee Milford). There was also valuable material in 'Two Brothers, A Milford Memoir' by Theodore Richard Milford, a cousin of Mrs Ridler.

2. DAKERS, C *Clouds, The Biography of a Country House* YaleUniversity Press, New Haven & London 1993 p116.

3. *The Story of Mere* by a Committee of Mere people, Blackmore Press, Gillingham (Dorset) 1958.

4. SIDWELL, E & M *Mere Museum Monographs No. 5* Friends of Mere Museum 1995

5. *Articles of a Benefit Society held at the Black Horse Inn, East Knoyle in the County of Wilts called THE UNION SOCIETY, established the 14th day of June 1810* Printed by C Bastable, Bookseller, Shaftesbury 1870.

Work and Play

References:

1. COLT HOARE, R *History of Modern Wiltshire* 1822, quoted by PLATT, J.R.I. - see below.

2. PLATT, J.R.I. For a full history of the South & West Wilts Hunt *see Three Hundred Years of Foxhunting in South and West Wiltshire* Berkswell Publishing, Warminster, 1990.

Peace and War

References:

East Knoyle Parish Magazine 1911.

History of the Wiltshire Home Guard 1940-44. W.R.O. 30989.

Ghosts?

The recollections described have been provided by present and former residents of the village.

Seven Notable Knoylians

Sources: The W.I. Scrapbooks (which include a number of press obituaries), the late Mrs Alice Beard, Mrs E.M. Roberts, Miss Marion Littlecott, Mrs Joan Jesse, Mr Cliford Sully and the late Mr Alfred Tanswell.

The People and the Place

Sources: The W.I. Scrapbooks Vols I-III; The Village Scrapbooks, Vols. IV & V; the Parish Registers; The Victoria County History Vol. XI.

Index

Note: References in **bold** type are to illustrations.